T0248435

JARVIS CC

Jarvis Cocker is a musician and broadcaster from the north of England. He formed the band Pulp in 1978 while at secondary school. They went on to become one of the most successful British groups of the 1990s. Between 2009 and 2017 he presented the BBC 6 Music programme *Jarvis Cocker's Sunday Service* as well as the ongoing, award-winning BBC Radio 4 documentary series *Wireless Nights*. He has honorary doctorates from Sheffield Hallam University and Central Saint Martin's School of Art (which he attended 1988–91). His lyric collection *Mother, Brother, Lover* was published by Faber in 2011. *Good Pop, Bad Pop* is his first work of long-form prose. He divides his time between Paris, London and the Peak District. His star sign is Virgo.

JARVIS COCKER

Good Pop, Bad Pop

An Inventory

(Designed by Julian House)

VINTAGE

3 5 7 9 10 8 6 4

Vintage is part of the Penguin Random House group of companies whose
addresses can be found at global.penguinrandomhouse.com.

Copyright © Jarvis Cocker 2022

First published in Vintage in 2023
First published in hardback by Jonathan Cape in 2022

penguin.co.uk/vintage

A CIP catalogue record for this book is available from the British Library

ISBN 9781784707910

Typeset in 8.93/12.6 pt Sabon LT Pro by Jouve UK, Milton Keynes
Printed and bound in Latvia by Livonia Print

The authorised representative in the EEA is Penguin Random House Ireland,
Morrison Chambers, 32 Nassau Street, Dublin D02 YH68

Penguin Random House is committed to a sustainable future for
our business, our readers and our planet. This book is made from
Forest Stewardship Council® certified paper.

To K.S., for letting it happen again,
&
Jeannette, for making it happen always.

Chapter One

There was a house I lived in for a while.
I stored a lot of stuff in the loft of this house.

When I say 'stored a lot of stuff' that's really a polite way of saying 'used it as a skip'. I crammed things into this loft space willy-nilly over a period of time – just to get them out of the way. Out of sight, out of mind. Then it all stayed up there for about twenty years because I wasn't living in London any more. I was living in Paris & various other places.

It played on my mind from time to time, this loft. I couldn't really put my finger on why it bothered me, but I knew it was something I would need to deal with one day. But that 'one day' never seemed to come around.

You could think of this loft as a manifestation of the way a modern human being accumulates stuff almost unconsciously.

Or you could think of it as a bin that's never been emptied.

Circumstances have finally dictated that I now have no choice but to clear out this loft.

The day of reckoning is upon me.

So let's get to it.

I have decided that, rather than simply take it all to the dump, I will look at every single item & then make an 'informed' decision as to whether to keep it or not.

Why?

Because I know that there's something important in here somewhere. Some kind of life story, some kind of revelation – but we're going to have to dig for it. I'm not using the royal 'we' – I'd like you to help me.

I won't make you look at every single thing I find in here – that would take for ever – but it feels important to have a witness. We can even make a game out of it – let's call it 'Keep or Cob'. ('Cob' being a Sheffield word meaning 'to throw', e.g. 'I cobbed it at a kid.')

AUTHOR'S NOTE:

When I use the word "loft" you may be mentally picturing a space where we can stand up & investigate in comfort together. This is not the case. The photo on the cover of this book is a stock image selected for design purposes – it does not show the loft I am writing about. My "loft" is a storage space accessed via a hatch set into the wall of a room on the top floor of a house built in Victorian times. The space is just over three feet in height at the point of entry & slopes down to nothing where the roof meets the façade of the house. It runs the entire width of the house, which is a distance of twenty-five feet or so. If you were to imagine being inside a giant Toblerone packet you would be getting close to a picture of the environment we are exploring. There is no way we can stand up. The only way to look at things is to crawl into the space, wriggle through the dust & cobwebs & bring a few items back into the main room to be photographed & inspected. It feels like mining: it's dirty, uncomfortable & awkward work.

You can see that it's just one big jumble. When I first poked my head in here, I discovered pretty quickly that there was no rhyme or reason to it. I know there must be some useful or interesting items. Some of the objects date back all the way to my childhood, but there's no way to access them because of there being so much crap in here as well. That's why I'm going to have to look at every single thing before I decide whether to throw it away or not. I don't want to miss something important. & I've learnt over the years that the most important things in life are not always immediately obvious.

OK, enough scene-setting: close your eyes, stick your hand in that pile over there & see what you come up with . . .

5

This is Extra gum when it was still in stick form. It hadn't evolved into its present 'tablet' state yet. This is twenty-year-old gum. Unused. Unchewed. For years I have carried a packet of chewing gum in the right-hand pocket of my jacket at all times. It was an essential part of my parenting. It has to be peppermint. Spearmint is too sweet. Fruit flavours are an abomination. But this packet pre-dates my parenthood. This is the chewing gum of a single man.

This is actually a good place to start because it proves that we could find anything up here. You might have been expecting piles of precious manuscripts & decaying master tapes (we'll get to those later) – a peek into a self-curated creative archive. But it's going to be more like sifting through a landfill (or would it be better to call it a 'mindfill'?). This *is* an archive of sorts & maybe that will become apparent as we go along. In the meantime: I've no idea why this chewing gum is here – it's not like I have a chewing-gum loft the way other people have a wine cellar – but here it is: we've found it & we've contemplated it. It's worth a photo but not worth keeping. The vintage Wrigley's Extra gum goes in the bin. Or in other words: COB. (My word, I feel so fresh.)

Next item: a sew-on Wigan Casino patch. Wigan Casino was the epicentre of the Northern Soul scene in the mid '70s. I was too young to experience it first-hand myself but I remember older boys coming to school with the 'look': really high-waisted trousers that were mega-flared. Feather-cut hair. I once got kicked in the teeth at a teenage party when someone did a swallow dive too near to me in the very confined space of their living room.

But I must have picked this up later in life – those '5 Soulful Years' ended when I was fifteen. I appreciated Northern Soul more in retrospect. It was a proper subculture – a spontaneous invention: people in the north of England dancing all night to obscure Black American Soul records from the previous decade. I may have been too young to fully appreciate the scene at the time but the idea of music being an almost life-or-death, secret-society kind of pursuit lodged in my mind. This patch is definitely more substantial than the chewing gum – as in: I can discern a reason for me having kept hold of it. Still can't remember how it came into my possession though. It's Psychic Lint – something you pick up without realising. We'll be coming across rather a lot of that.

Keep or cob? That's more difficult than last time – but seeing as I've owned it for at least thirty years & never sewn it on to anything I think it's time to let go: I'll give it to someone who might appreciate it more.

Like you, for instance? (Consider it a bribe.)

Wow. Collar supports. I have never knowingly used collar supports. Perhaps I thought I might need them in later life – my collars might start going floppy with age or something. That doesn't appear to have happened yet (thank you, Lord) so this one is easy: COB.

OK – I have to admit to a bit of stage-managing here: I wouldn't want to lose you this early in the book so here's a bit of 'juice'. This was the first thing I spotted up here that convinced me it could be worth entering into this process of self-excavation, rather taking the entire contents of the loft to the nearest public dump. This is a school exercise book (originally belonging to my mother according to the name written at the top) in which the fifteen-year-old me wrote his ideas about being in a band. I can't believe I found this. This book documents the very first attempts to kick-start my creativity. Now we're talking.

Because, as well as being a kind of house-clearance catalogue, this is also going to be a book about the creative process – specifically *my* creative process. Not a 'self-help' or 'how to' guide but, as it is my belief that all human beings have the creative gene within them, I'm hoping to shed a little light on how the process works. For everyone. You're making creative decisions every minute of the day. Yes, you are. I'll prove it.

But now, back to the exercise book . . .

My chosen mode of artistic expression is pop music.

Like pretty much every other kid of my generation I had been a pop-music fan almost since birth – & when I hit my teens I wanted to make the jump from spectator to participant. Big jump. So this exercise book is a very important document. It's my Dead Sea Scrolls – the beginning of my artistic journey – & it begins with . . .

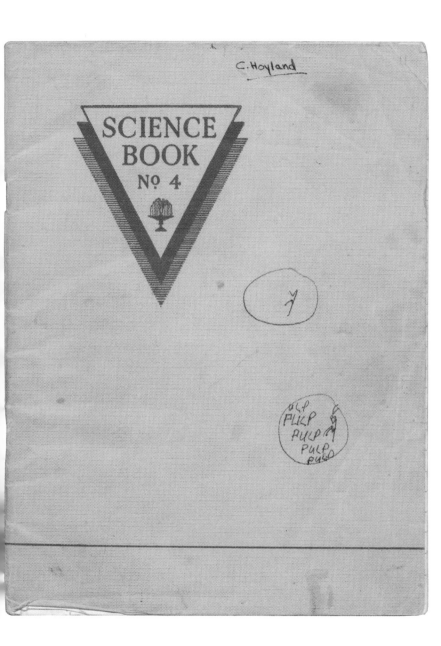

SCIENCE
BOOK
No 4

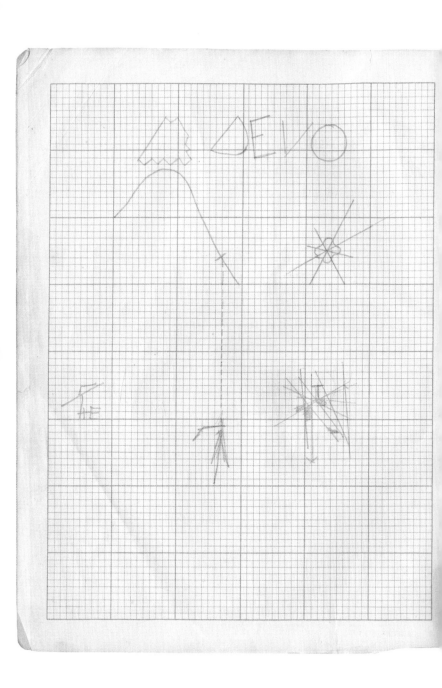

Pulp Fashion

Most Groups have a certain mode of dress which is invariably emulated by their followers. The Pulp Wardrobe shall consist of :-

Duffle Coats (preferably blue or black)

Crew-neck jumpers (of the "rancid" (S.A type, or of woollen or cotton construction)

Garishly (preferably day-glo) coloured T and Sweat shirts preferably of an abstract design.

"Fungus"-style t-shirts. (sans cap + sleeves)

Plain-coloured shirts (no patterns)

Rancid ties.

Drainpipe or tapered-trousers preferably of a colourful disposition.

Pointy boots.

Cheapo white baseball boots.

Oxfam Jackets (preferably with button-holes) Jackets made of strange materials (e.g. polythene, wood)

Silly Socks.

Hair = Shortish (not skinhead) (No sequins unless for silly purposes)

Pulp Wardrobe (illustrated)

Crew-Neck Jumper

Garish T-Shirt

Pale Blue

Pink

Purple

Yellow

Duffle

Optional

Green

Plain Shirt

Rancid Tie

Mauve

Drainpipe Trousers

Pointy Boob

Buttonhole

Cheapo White Baseball Boob

Silly Socks

A sequin being OK used for a silly purpose

Oxfam (or Paper) Jacket

Hair (Shortish)

. . . clothes.

'Most Groups have a certain mode of dress which is invariably emulated by their followers. The Pulp Wardrobe shall consist of . . .'

'A bloody fashion guide?' That was my first reaction on reading these words. But that's the me of today thinking. This is hard evidence. Primary sources. Original artefacts. It all counts. No argument. Even the chewing gum (maybe *especially* the chewing gum).

Up here we're going to meet the past on its own terms. No revisionism. So look again: what can this guide to 'Pulp Fashion' possibly tell us?

Well, it places image at the very forefront of this impending creative adventure.

That's similar to the Northern Soul scene we touched upon during our contemplation of that Wigan Casino patch just a moment ago – but, more significantly for me, Punk Rock had happened only a couple of years before I wrote this style guide.

I'm assuming that if you're reading this book you will already be fairly familiar with the story of punk. You might even be sick of hearing about it. There are loads of books on the subject. & documentaries. & blogs. & Facebook groups. This is a Modern Problem: the way things get the life sucked out of them by repetition & assimilation into the mainstream – but this is especially unfortunate in the case of punk.

Because punk was a rupture. A complete break with the past. A rejection of the official narrative. It didn't want to fit in. It demanded new sounds, new ideas. & new clothes.

Punk stressed the importance of dress as a way of pledging your allegiance to the New World Order – of signifying your distaste for the 'straight' world. Not 'dress to impress' more 'dress to disgust'.

There's not much to disgust the average man on the street in the 'Pulp Wardrobe' though: no safety pins or PVC.

The Pulp Fashion Revolution will feature:

Duffel coats (preferably blue or black): I'd been bought a duffel coat by my Aunty Bess. That's about as square as it gets. & duffel coats are made of thick, woollen material so they definitely wouldn't be very practical as stage-wear.

Crew-neck jumper (of the 'rancid' C&A type): There was a big C&A store in the centre of Sheffield. These jumpers were 100 per cent acrylic & very cheap. Went bobbly really fast. Still a bit warm for stage-wear.

Garish T-shirt: The one vaguely 'punk' influence in the list. I think I had conducted some home-dyeing experiments.

Plain-coloured shirt (no pattern): This rule didn't last very long.

Rancid tie: 'Rancid' seems to have been one of my favourite words at this stage in my life.

Drainpipe (or tapered) trousers: I'm surprised by tapered trousers making the list. We had a history teacher at school called Mr Marsden who wore suits with extremely tapered trousers. We referred to them as 'shit-stoppers'.

Pointy boots & Cheapo white baseball boots: Both from an Army Stores near Sheffield's Castle Market.

Hair (shortish): Cutting your hair was the quickest & easiest way of signifying you had 'gone punk'. My sister cut mine. Ended up with quite a few bald patches.

These are not 'punk' clothes – in fact, most of them are just slight variations on the school uniform I had to wear every day. Minor adjustments barely perceptible to a casual bystander – nothing that could get me detention – but I knew they were important. I was starting to do my own thing.

Punk happened at such an important time for me: I was just hitting adolescence. I'd wanted to be in a band since the age of seven but I had no clue how to go about it. It felt about as realistic as my other childhood ambition: to be an astronaut. I thought it probably required a diploma. Some kind of academic achievement that was beyond my reach.

I remember asking for *The Beatles Illustrated Song Book* for Christmas one year & then being dismayed by how every song had so many chords in it. We had an acoustic guitar that my mum had bought as an ornament while at college & I would sit looking at the pages of the book & then at my fingers on the fretboard, feeling totally helpless. Then punk arrived & there was that famous slogan on the front of some fanzine that said, 'This is a chord. This is another. This is a third. Now form a band.' It was absolutely perfect timing – learning three chords was achievable (just about) – plus, punk was saying that there was more to music than mere ability: in fact, ability was part of the problem. Attitudes & beliefs were key too. What a song was ABOUT was as important as how it sounded. If not more so. The main thing was that it had to be exciting. I reckoned I could get with that. Plus, it wouldn't require as much effort as having to learn an instrument 'properly'.

A closer look at the exercise book illustrates my situation perfectly. There's a scribbled attempt by me to write out a piece of music. I've never been able to read or write music in the conventional manner – crotchets & quavers & all that – so this was the best I could do. Now I've just gone downstairs to get a guitar to work out what song this is. & I now realise these are the chords to 'Annie's Song' by John Denver. ('You fill up my senses', etc.) Wow.

Credibility. Blown.

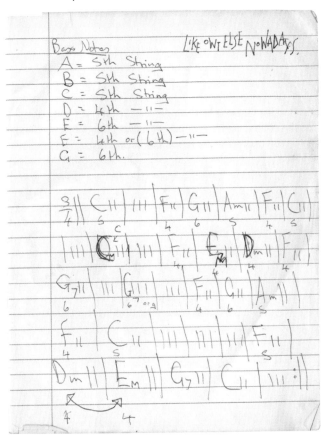

Come to think of it, I do now remember that I once attended a night-school class in 'beginner's guitar' at a Further Education college up the road from our house, & diligently copied these chords down when the teacher showed us them. I remember him doing it in a disdainful manner because 'Annie's Song' had been a hit & he thought it was corny, but I was all for it. It wasn't that I was a massive John Denver fan, but after my Beatles Humiliation I was desperate to be able to play something & it actually be recognisable as a song. I wanted to join in at all costs. Even if it meant embracing The Denver.

Then, punk came along & rendered this effort obsolete. Saved me from a life of finger-picking. Showed me another way. Another world. A world of dancing & shouting & laughing.

& clothes.

What a relief. There might also be another reason I began this creative manifesto with a wardrobe guide, though. Up to this point in my life I'd been bought all my clothes by my mum & other relatives. & this had caused me some distress.

The most painfully extreme example being when my uncle John's German in-laws sent over a pair of lederhosen as a gift for me when I was about seven. They were made out of grey suede with bottle-green leather edging & had matching braces featuring a bone carving of a stag across the chest. I looked like an Alpine goatherd in them. But my mum thought it would be fine for me to go to school looking like this. As soon as I entered the school yard the hilarity began – & it only increased when a classmate noticed that there were two zip fasteners on the front of the shorts. A new insult was added to the all-too-familiar 'Four Eyes' – I was now Jarvis 'Two Dicks'. As I said: distressing.

Experiences such as this meant I longed to be able to blend into the background & not draw attention to myself. I was also embarrassed by my name – I remember going on a city-wide Cub Scout camping weekend & telling the head Scoutmaster that my name was John just to avoid having to say 'Jarvis' in

public. My friends stared at me quizzically – then I had to keep up the pretence the whole weekend. More distress.

So that's another reason I breathed such a sigh of relief when punk happened: finally, I could relax & stop being so uptight about having a funny name. Punk performers gave themselves funny names on purpose! Johnny Rotten, Captain Sensible, Lux Interior, Gaye Advert, Johnny Moped . . . I was actually one step ahead of them because I didn't even have to change mine.

Starting my creative journey with the 'Pulp Wardrobe' now makes perfect sense to me. It's attainable. It is me saying, 'From now on I'm going to do my own thing – I might not know exactly what "my own thing" is yet, but I'm going to find out.' Punk gave me the confidence & permission to join in. & clothes were a very quick way of pledging allegiance whilst trying to work out what to do next. I hadn't got a band yet – but at least I knew what that band was going to look like when I did. Clothes got the ball rolling. Get the costumes made & then find the people to wear them. Very *Field of Dreams*.

We'll come back to this exercise book later – but now I think it's time for us to take another item from the pile . . .

Chapter Two

The penny has dropped – well, a
halfpenny, at least. A halfpenny coin
set in epoxy resin if we want
to be totally precise.

Setting things in clear resin was a popular hobby in the '70s. You could buy a kit called Plasticraft. Kids made their own paperweights & brooches, with seashells & clock parts suspended in clear plastic – like that insect preserved for ever in a drop of amber in *Jurassic Park*. The fumes produced as the resin 'cured' were incredibly toxic. Probably many kids' gateway into solvent abuse. I think this is half of a set of cufflinks. Don't know where the other one is – & the bit that goes through the shirt cuffs has broken off. On the whole, a pretty obsolete object – one for the COB pile?

Well, hold on a minute: everything has to be considered in full, remember? I never had a Plasticraft kit as a child – I coveted one but never owned one – so that must mean that I bought this cufflink at some point. Why would I do that? To own something I was denied as a child? That can't be the whole story. It's a coin of the realm made into a piece of male jewellery . . . Remind you of anything?

Well, have you ever seen a man wearing a pair of gold sovereign cufflinks?

At the time of writing gold sovereigns are worth about £400 each. So you'd be walking around with going on for a Grand poking out through your sleeves if you wore a pair. They're a status symbol. A 'Flash Harry' statement. Considered a bit naff now. But, back in the day, a sign that you'd made it – & you were flaunting it.

That's why the halfpence cufflinks appealed to me back then: as a punk statement. A 'lack-of-status' symbol. A small rebellion against the values of the 'straight' world I'd now decided I was against. This is a Rebel Cufflink.

Definitely a KEEPer.

This pile of plastic novelties say 'Pulp' to me. Bright. Shiny. Mass-produced. The type of thing you might find in a Christmas cracker. But I considered them precious. Take a closer look at the picture: we've got ① Father Christmas, ② sport, ③ smoking, ④ marriage, ⑤ kindness to animals & ⑥ death. All human life is there – in pop form. (Pop and Pulp are interchangeable terms for me.)

The name 'Pulp' came early on. I've often told the story that I was in an economics lesson at school when we were given a copy of the *Financial Times* & my eye was caught by 'Arabicus Pulp' in the Commodities section of the paper. (I think it's something to do with coffee.) That's a true story – but 'Pulp' was the important bit for me.

Because the idea that a culture could reveal more of itself through its throwaway items than through its supposedly revered artefacts was fascinating to me. Still is.

More KEEPers, I'm afraid.

I'm now holding a shirt. It's orange with white circles on it. 'Prova' is embroidered on the label. I think that was the home brand of British Home Stores.

This is a 'Gold Star' shirt. That might have had something to do with why I bought it. More positive visualisation. But the main reason I'm showing you this is that, as far as I remember (fanfare, please), this is the first second-hand clothing item I ever bought.

That was a big step for me. I got into buying second-hand clothes because just one hundred yards away from the family home was a Methodist church, & they had jumble sales in their church hall from time to time. & my discovery of jumble sales pretty much coincided with my discovery of punk.

The nearest thing to jumble sales in the present day are car boot sales, but the atmosphere is substantially different at a car boot sale. At jumble sales people donate their unwanted items so they can be re-sold to raise money for a new church roof or whatever. At a car boot sale the sellers are hoping to personally benefit from selling their items. The philanthropic element is absent. Plus, programmes such as *Antiques Roadshow* have made customers think they might stumble across a priceless masterpiece they can sell on at auction for millions. So the atmosphere can be a little 'charged'. I remember once seeing a guy at a car boot sale turn over a vase so that he could look at the maker's mark on the bottom – he must have seen an expert do that on telly – & all this slop that looked like a discarded Pot Noodle slid out of the vase & down his sleeve. That kind of sums up car boot sales for me.

Jumble sales were much mellower. & they were such a source of inspiration to my younger self. The message taken from punk was that 'it's OK to look different'. I was no longer going to try (& fail) to fit in – so from now on I was going to buy my own clothes. The only problem with this resolution was that I didn't actually have any money. I mean, I *was* doing a paper round. So I was earning maybe £2 a week. But, even allowing for inflation, I think you can tell that wasn't going to go very far in funding my Extreme Makeover.

So jumble sales really were a godsend. They were cheap. Incredibly cheap, really. You generally had to pay 5p to get in, & then individual items would be somewhere between 10 & 20p each. Affordable. You could get a whole new wardrobe for under a pound. & because the clothes were so cheap you could really experiment. Take a leap in the dark. You could see something & think, 'Well, it's only 10p, so I'll buy it & see what it looks like when I get home. Maybe a batwing jumper will really suit me.'

Jumble sales were also where I discovered my hunter-gatherer instinct. You had to dive into these big piles of clothing along with everyone else & just rummage around until you found something that took your fancy. It could get pretty physical. You had to think fast if you didn't want to leave empty-handed. Steep learning curve for a shy teenager.

It certainly beat going to a regular shop – apart from the price aspect, I'd never particularly liked going to shops anyway, especially clothes shops – because the assistants would invariably want to talk to you & sometimes even follow you around the shop when all you wanted to do was browse in peace. Plus, normal shops now seemed boring in comparison to jumble sales. Everything just hanging there meekly on a clothes rail. You didn't have to fight a gang of old women to get to what you wanted. Pretty tame.

& where were the refreshments? Tea was available at a very reasonable price at a jumble sale. & home-made cake. It was a scene. A complete day out. For a quid or so.

So, I'm glad I still have this. The first shirt that I ever bought from a jumble sale. It contravenes the Shirt Rule as featured in the Pulp Manifesto: 'plain-coloured shirts (no patterns)' (told you that rule didn't last very long), but that doesn't matter, it marks the dawn of a new sensibility.

Because as well as getting myself something to wear, I was also now taking society's cast-offs & 're-purposing' them. I was learning about the world by looking at what it threw away. By what it deemed 'worthless'. This was the real beginning of the Pulp aesthetic. Sifting through the debris to find an alternative to the official narrative. Using second-hand items to tell a brand-new story.

To tell my own story. Which is pretty much the definition of the creative act, as far as I can make out.

On that same day I also bought a nylon attempt at a Fair Isle jumper in green, white & black which my mother was so appalled by that I had to keep it hidden away under my bed.

But there was no hiding the truth:

The Grand Experiment had begun

A SEXY LAUGHS Special!

THE FANTASTIC DIRTY JOKE BOOK

ONE GOLDTOP TOP FLOOR PLEASE

FORBES.

Chapter Three

I wouldn't want you to get the impression that my teenage concerns were purely creative . . . there were procreative ones too.

A group of businessmen visited a new rubber manufacturing plant. In one department the machines were making a noise that sounded like BOOM S-ss.

"Here we make baby nipples," explained the guide. "When you hear the BOOM, the pistons force the mechanical mould into the rubber, making a perfect nipple. The S-ss which follows is the sound made when the machine perforates the nipple."

In the next department, the sound from the machines was a BOOM, BOOM, BOOM, BOOM, S-ss. "In this section we manufacture male contraceptives," said the guide.

"What's the S-ss sound for?" asked one of the men.

"Oh, that," replied the guide, "well, we perforate every fifth one to make sure there is a demand for baby nipples!"

"Sure, I remember you now—You were one of the girls at Madam Duval's!"

What I'm holding here is a *Sexy Laughs Fantastic Dirty Joke Book*. I've had this in my possession for even longer than the Prova Gold Star shirt. & it's a key factor in my sexual development. Seriously. Let me tell you how I got hold of it.

School used to send us for swimming lessons in the centre of Sheffield. I'd have been around thirteen or fourteen years old: post-pubescent but pre-punk. The lessons were at a place called Sheaf Valley Baths, which was right next to the bus station. We did things like picking up a rubber brick from the bottom of the pool & treading water in our pyjamas (the latter would come in useful if you were ever on a ship & happened to sleepwalk overboard).

There was always a rush to get upstairs & sit on the back seat of the bus back to school because, as anyone with any sense knows, they're the best seats in the house. One day when we got upstairs this magazine was lying there waiting for us.

You can imagine the excitement it caused among a bunch of teenage boys. A furtive glimpse into the adult world. A sneak peek. It was passed around from hand to hand & then there was a bit of a fight over who was going to keep hold of it when we got off the bus. You can tell there was a tussle because the back cover has been ripped off.

The fact that it's up here in the loft means that I must have somehow won that tussle & taken it home with me. Difficult to believe – I certainly wasn't the 'hardest' kid in the class – but here's the evidence. Perhaps the tough kids realised my need was greater than theirs.

I was desperate to find out about sex. Or perhaps I should qualify that statement: I was desperate to find out about sex from a MALE perspective.

Perhaps this picture gives you some idea of why I say that. Here I am at the age of seven, surrounded by my immediate family. My mum, my grandma, my sister, my aunties Mandy & Jutta – a very feminine environment (even Nif the cat was female).

My father had left home that year, & my mother's brother had died just a few months earlier. The only constant male presence left in the family was my grandfather (he took the photo) & he just seemed . . . old. I couldn't imagine him & my grandma having sex. Did not want that image in my mind. So when I got home from school I used to eavesdrop on my mum & her female friends chatting in the kitchen, hoping to pick up some clues. Often they would talk about the men in their lives. This was a hot topic seeing as all their husbands were gone for one reason or another. A conversation that really stuck in my mind was when one of them was talking about how she was going to 'pack' her boyfriend because he was too 'nice'. That was a difficult concept to get my head round at the time because, as a kid, you're always being told to be 'nice'. By adults. But now it seemed that rule didn't always apply when you were grown up. There were exceptions – times when niceness could be a drawback. Mixed messages. Sex was confusing. I was hoping the *Sexy Laughs Fantastic Dirty Joke Book* might shed light on a few matters. As far as I knew, only men read (or wrote) dirty magazines so here was a chance for me to hear the other side of the story.

I was in for a disappointment. First off, I didn't really get any of the jokes. For instance:

• • •

Did you hear about the bridge expert who became the father of twins? His wife doubled his bid.

• • •

What the hell was this supposed to mean? Now I know it's a weak joke involving card games – but at the time I thought it was code for some kind of sexual act. I mean, a bridge connects two pieces of land so could this be referring to some way of connecting two people? Logical? I was clueless.

Another time I was messing around on the swings in a playground with a friend when some older girls asked us if we masturbated. When I got home I took our dictionary down off the shelf & looked up the definition of 'masturbate'. I was informed that it meant 'to abuse oneself'. So for a while I thought that masturbation meant calling yourself rude names. Walking around shouting at yourself 'shithead!' or 'fart!' or something like that.

Yet another source of confusion came from the local public toilet. There was a lot of graffiti in there. What was I meant to make of these immortal lines?

> *Once I saw a right shag*
> *It sat upon a wall*
> *I tried to put my jonny on*
> *& strangled my left ball.*

I knew it must have something to do with sex but I had no clue as to its meaning except that 'strangling' your left ball sounded very unpleasant. Sex could also be dangerous. & the fact that you had to look for information about it in places that reeked of piss didn't bode well.

If anything, the *Sexy Laughs Fantastic Dirty Joke Book* only added to my state of confusion: because I didn't understand the jokes in it, I assumed I didn't understand anything about sex itself.

Now I realise they are just crap jokes.

The book also features some black-&-white images of semi-naked women.

At least these had a *practical* use.

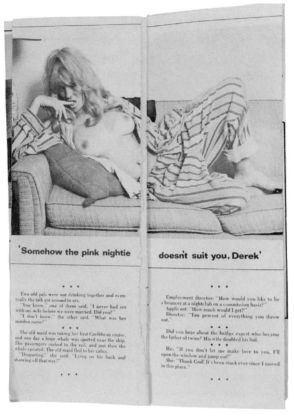

'Somehow the pink nightie doesn't suit you, Derek'

* * *

Two old pals were out drinking together and eventually the talk got around to sex.
"You know," one of them said, "I never had sex with my wife before we were married. Did you?"
"I don't know," the other said. "What was her maiden name?"

* * *

The old maid was taking her first Caribbean cruise, and one day a huge whale was spotted near the ship. The passengers rushed to the rail, and just then the whale spouted. The old maid fled to her cabin.
"Disgusting!" she said. "Lying on his back and showing off that way!"

* * *

Employment director: "How would you like to be a bouncer at a nightclub on a commission basis?"
Applicant: "How much would I get?"
Director: "Ten percent of everything you throw out."

* * *

Did you hear about the bridge expert who became the father of twins? His wife doubled his bid.

* * *

He: "If you don't let me make love to you, I'll open the window and jump out!"
She: "Thank God! It's been stuck ever since I moved in this place."

* * *

I first rediscovered this book around the time my son was going through puberty (there have been earlier, unsuccessful attempts to grapple with the contents of The Loft, oh yes) & I thought, 'Well, my father wasn't around to give me a "birds & bees" talk but why shouldn't I give one?' I had been so needy of information back then. I had made a pact with myself that it was something I would do for my son when the time came. Step up to the plate.

I thought I could use this book as an ice-breaker to broach the subject of sex & attitudes to women. I think a lot of modern parents feel a real icy dread when their kids are approaching puberty. We are living in the age of Google. & if a kid types in search words such as 'sex' – or 'naked women' or even '*once I saw a right shag, it sat upon a wall . . .*' – there's a good chance that they are going to end up looking at some pretty unsavoury material.

It was freaking me out that my son's first introduction to the world of sex might be looking at something really explicit or foul online.

So out came the *Sexy Laughs Fantastic Dirty Joke Book* – & a rather awkward conversation began.

I told him how I'd found the magazine when I was around his age & starting to get curious about sex. I wanted to get across to him that it's natural to look for information about sex – but what you're going to find won't necessarily be an accurate depiction of what sex is like between two real people. I told him about my frustration at not being able to 'get' the jokes in the *Sexy Laughs Fantastic Dirty Joke Book*. What you see online (or find on the back seat of the bus) are *ideas* about sex. Or material that takes the place of sex for a certain demographic. The main thrust of my argument was that viewing online material or looking at porno mags is not a good 'entry point' (if you'll pardon the phrase) to the world of sexual relationships. Sex is a thing that two people do together. Not something you do *to* someone but *with* someone.

End of lecture.

There was a short silence & then my son laughed for quite a long time & said that I could have saved my breath because they'd already told them all about sex at school. That also conjured up some horrific images for me.

In the one single sex-education class we had during my schooldays they showed us the 'sex act' in diagram form, followed by some close-up photos of the effects of sexually transmitted diseases & then topped the whole thing off with an extremely graphic film of a woman giving birth, shot from the 'business' end. I fainted when the baby's head popped out. The whole programme appeared to have been designed to put kids off sex for life. Nearly worked.

I tried to convince my son that there was also a lot more to sex than mere 'technicalities' but I could tell he was losing interest. So I informed him that there were some condoms under the bathroom sink & left it at that.

But the *Sexy Laughs Fantastic Dirty Joke Book* had finally earned its keep. It gave me a place to start that father–son conversation. Perhaps that conversation was more important to the father than the son – but that's beside the point: it happened. KEEP.

Some of the stuff up here in the loft might turn out to be useful after all.

Imagine that.

Chapter Four

It would be comforting to think that what I've been doing all these years is squirrelling away a store of items that will be of use to me one day.

Then we come across an item like the one on the previous page. Firstly, I'm irritated by the fact that I don't know what this object actually is. It looks like it ought to be a keyring but I don't see how you would get keys on to that stirrup-shaped thing the leather strap is attached to. Any ideas? Then there's the slogan: 'LOVE ME, I'M NICE AND EASY'. Did I really aspire to being 'nice & easy' to love at some point? Or did I think it would be hilariously inappropriate to advertise myself as such? I could have been prosecuted under the Trades Description Act.

I still haven't worked out what it is after twenty years so I'm damned if I'm going to hang on to it any longer. COB.

This looks more promising. A Sterling Electric multi-band radio. It's got an impressive-looking dial & map panel that allows you to work out what time it is in any part of the world. Plus, it's got a 'squelch' control.

I listened to the radio from an early age, but didn't see a live band until I was thirteen. The five-year-old me therefore believed that music was something that came out perfectly formed & pre-prepared from a small box on the shelf in the kitchen. (If I'd been born back in the 1700s maybe there would have been a weird uncle who came round & played his penny whistle over my crib every now & then. & that would have been my first experience of music. Frightening thought.)

Coming into the world when I did, the radio WAS music as far as I was concerned. Specifically pop radio. Some of my earliest memories are of getting ready for primary school with the radio on in the background. Terry Wogan presented the *Breakfast Show*. I had a vivid picture in my mind of him being a blonde-haired man in a cream Aran jumper. That's the image I'd created purely based on hearing the sound of his voice. It was a shock when I eventually got to see the 'real' him during his *Blankety Blank* period.

If you're brought up in a household where the radio is on constantly, then whatever is playing will go in there & stay put & become part of the bedrock of your personality. All these years later my image of Terry Wogan as an Aran jumper-clad blonde man still feels more genuine than the photos I've subsequently seen of him because that self-generated image pre-dates all others. It's my Primal Wogan.

One of the first songs I remember hearing on the radio is 'Where Do You Go To My Lovely?' by Peter Sarstedt which was a Number 1 hit in the UK for four weeks in 1969. The bit of the song that really got to me was a line in the chorus where he sang, 'I can see inside your head.' The idea that a stranger communicating with you via the radio might be able to do that both excited & terrified me. It made me feel that a song was a kind of magic trick. (& I was right.)

At the age of five I had no inkling what the words to 'Where Do You Go To My Lovely?' meant. Who were Marlene Dietrich & Zizi Jeanmaire? Where was the Boulevard St Michel or Juan-les-Pins? & how did you sip Napoleon brandy without getting your lips wet? But, despite the fact that I had no real idea what all these things Peter Sarstedt was singing about were, I did understand something very important about his song: it gave me The Tingle.

The Tingle is fundamental to my creative story. The Tingle is what led to me writing my own songs.

People have different ways of referring to this feeling. Some say 'chills' (that makes me think of *Grease*). Other people say 'goosebumps' (I associate that more with being scared shitless). But it all means the same thing: you're having a physical reaction to music. For me it's a tingling sensation around the top of my shoulders & the back of my neck.

I don't experience The Tingle in any other art form. Or rather, it may happen occasionally – but with music it happens a lot.

In fact, it's what I'm searching for when I listen to a new piece of music because it's a very pleasant feeling to have. I liked experiencing this mysterious feeling. As a child I wanted to feel it more often. Eventually it made me want to try & make it happen to other people.

Those pop songs like 'Where Do You Go To My Lovely?' that played in our house when I was a kid were the first music that gave me The Tingle. So pop music was 'real' music as far as

I was concerned. The medium through which I discovered how music works & how it can make you feel. Over the years I've come to realise that this isn't the case for everyone.

For example:

In 2008 I recorded an album in Chicago with Steve Albini at his studio Electrical Audio. Steve Albini has a reputation for being 'hard-line' & 'straight-edge'. He has a band called Shellac who don't believe in having a road-crew, so they move their own gear on & off stage. He studied journalism at one point (his article 'The Problem With Music' is a great read). He recorded Nirvana's *In Utero* album. Impressive résumé. I was pretty nervous to work with him – but that soon disappeared when we got to the studio because he was wearing overalls. Blue overalls like a car mechanic would wear, with 'Electrical Audio' written on the back. As far as he's concerned he's just another blue-collar worker doing an honest day's work. I liked him immediately.

During a lunch of 'gourmet' hot-dogs in a break from recording one day, he happened to ask me what my favourite type of music was. 'Pop music,' I replied, without really thinking. A look of absolute horror & disbelief came on his face: to him the term 'pop music' means cynically exploitative, mass-produced songs aimed at parting the kids from their cash as effectively as possible. It represents The Man at his absolute worst. Everything he hates about the music business. Steve Albini has been quoted as saying that 'pop music is for children & idiots'. Oops. I must be being sarcastic, he suggested.

But I really wasn't.

The chart pop I listened to from an early age had a massive effect on my creative development. & it was fun.

The UK Pop Charts used to be a crazy collision of rampant commerce & grass-roots democracy: people 'voted' by buying records & then watching their progress up the charts. It was a national pastime – I can even remember kids bringing radios to school so they could hear the midweek chart positions at break

time. That's taking an interest. It was absolutely mainstream &
commercial but also – crucially – anyone could take part. Strange
things could happen.

I'm thinking of a song like 'O Superman' by Laurie Anderson
which got to Number 2 in the UK Singles Chart in 1981. That
record is basically someone talking through a vocoder whilst
someone else repeats the word 'ah' for five minutes – if something
that strange & radical could be a chart hit then surely pop was a
positive influence: new & challenging ideas could enter mainstream
culture if enough people decided to buy the records & put them
there. Pop could expand (& blow) minds.

Whether a record was a hit or not was determined by the
public. Labels could 'push' a single as hard as they liked but the
final decision rested with the general population. Either you
bought it or you didn't. That was the magic of pop: it couldn't be
predicted. A hit had to have that mysterious 'something' that
caught the popular imagination.

A 'something' that cut through all preconceptions about
taste, cool, intelligence, class, race & touched some common
human aspect of UK citizens in the latter half of the twentieth
century. Dziga Vertov's dream of a self-generated proletarian art
form made manifest. In the record department of Woolworths.
Good pop.

You can detect some of this Revolutionary Pop Zeal in the school exercise book we looked at earlier. After the fashion guide. There's The Pulp Master Plan.

'The group shall work its way into the public eye by producing fairly conventional, yet slightly off-beat, pop songs. After gaining a well-known and commercially successful status the group can then begin to subvert and restructure both the music-business and music itself.' It's the old 'change the system from within' approach: Pop success as Trojan Horse. This is my younger self's way of reconciling pop ambitions with my newly found punk ideals. I'm quite impressed. & there's better yet to come.

THE FULP MASTER PLAN

Category A - Music

Being, first and foremost, a musical unit it is fitting that Fulp's first conquest should be of the music business. The group shall work its way into the public eye by producing fairly conventional, yet slightly off-beat, pop songs. After gaining a well-known and commercially successful status the group can then begin to subvert the music and restructure both the music-business and music itself.

(1) The Music Business

After releasing first single on own self-financed label the group shall be signed up, on a very short-time deal, to a major record company. After fulfilling their contract Fulp shall then use their amassed resources to set up their own record label and string

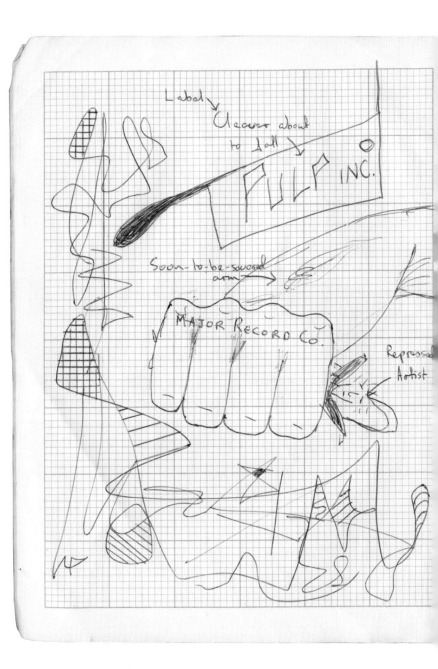

Label
Cleaver about
to fall

PULP INC.

Soon-to-be-severed
arm

MAJOR RECORD CO.

Repressed
Artist

Here's a diagram showing the way this is all going to work. Surely Mr Albini would approve.

A meat cleaver bearing the inscription 'PULP INC.' is about to fall & sever an arm with 'MAJOR RECORD CO.' written across the knuckles of its hand, & thus free the 'Repressed Artist' trapped in its fist.

I'm touched by the sentiment. A noble aim. Certainly more imaginative than aspiring to a Porsche & a big house. Bravo the fifteen-year-old me. From the very start I didn't see music purely as a form of entertainment – it could also be a way of changing the world. Punk, combined with the pop I'd heard on the radio as a kid, had created that sensibility. A heady brew.

But how was I going to get myself on the radio & thus kick-start the Tingle Revolution?

Chapter Five

Back to the jumble sale.
Back to the sifting.
Getting the hang of this now?

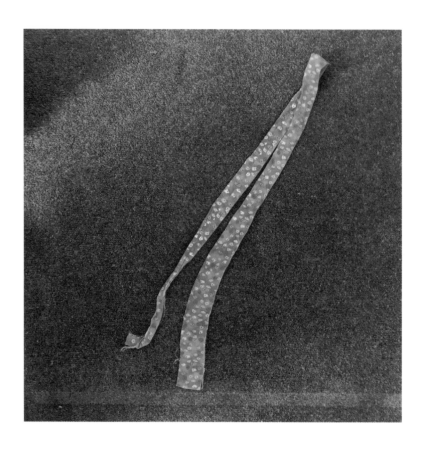

Item #5 on the Pulp Wardrobe list is 'Rancid Tie'. Here's a prime example. What am I bid? There's no label – it would appear to be home-made. Constructed from a cotton fabric featuring multicoloured flowers on an orange ground. Very frayed at the edges.

The fraying is because the owner wore it to school every day for about two years.

When I entered the sixth form certain rules on school uniform were relaxed. One of them being the wearing of the school tie. It was now optional. Most of my classmates stopped wearing ties altogether but I decided to come up with an alternative. The 'official' version had been thin diagonal red stripes on a bottle-green background. Regimented. Conventional. A budget version of the 'old school tie'. How about a New School Tie? How about wearing a bouquet of flowers round your neck every day instead? Now you're talking.

CITY SCHOOL
SHEFFIELD
1981
LOWER 6TH

Here's a school photo from 1981. I've been put on the back row with two other subversive tie-wearers. I'm seventeen now – it's a year or so since I wrote The Pulp Master Plan – the transformation is well under way.

School photos were the first time I can remember having my picture taken by a professional. I've done many photo sessions since but the basic rules have remained the same: first the group shot . . .

... & then the solo portrait

Which gives us the opportunity

... *to really study*

The Look

I've nailed my colours to the mast. The New School Tie is in place – & I've made my own Pulp badge especially for the photo-shoot. I now have Big Hair. The glasses have changed & there's something strange happening in the middle of my chin.

I've already started a group (at least in my own head). I made the decision to be a pop star. The manifesto has been written. Now I'm looking for clues on how to deliver on the 'core pledges'. How do I start to make it all happen? & is there anyone I can look to for guidance? School's a no-no: How To Be A Pop Star is not on the curriculum. I'm going to have to search elsewhere. In hindsight, my 'look' perfectly expresses the situation I now find myself in.

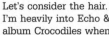

Let's consider the hair.

I'm heavily into Echo & the Bunnymen. I bought their debut album Crocodiles when it first came out in the summer of 1980. My favourite song on the record is called 'Rescue'.

I love the music but the image is important to me too. & foremost in that image is Ian McCulloch's hair. It's high. It's got volume. It's a godsend for a teenager with dry hair that tends towards 'bushiness'. I can now use my hair's natural unruliness to my advantage. Ian has shown the way. To paraphrase the song, he has 'come on down to my rescue'.

How about the thing on the chin? (I hesitate to call it a beard.)

The man on the left in this photo is Hugh Cornwell. He's the lead singer & guitarist with The Stranglers. I bought The Stranglers' debut album way back in the summer of 1977. It was the second album I ever bought. I hid it at the back of the record rack in case my mother disapproved of me having a 'punk' record. This is the back cover of a side project he made two years later. I didn't 'get' the record musically when i bought it, but now, in the summer of '81, it has finally come in handy. I've not been shaving very long. I have had to teach myself how to do it due to the continuing absence of male figures in my life. It's been a bloodbath. Aftershave really stings & seems to give you spots. How can I turn this major drag into a positive? I have a friend who is trying to grow a moustache so he can look like Freddie Mercury. It's taking some time. This weird little 'chin stripe' is much more easily attainable. & (in my mind) cool.

Looking at this photo on the rear sleeve of the Nosferatu album all these years later it crosses my mind that Hugh Cornwell's 'beard' might actually be a shadow cast by the cleft in his chin & not a beard at all. Surely not.

The glasses are the most obvious aspect of 'The Look'. People shout, 'Here comes Elvis Costello!' when I am walking through Sheffield city centre, or boarding a bus, or working at my Saturday job at the fish market. Buddy Holly, Roy Orbison &, on one occasion, Harold Lloyd (must have been a lippy pensioner) also crop up, but Elvis Costello is the runaway favourite. Especially since 'Oliver's Army' was a big hit in the spring of 1979.

At the time, National Health spectacles are available free for kids from one-parent families. They come in black or transparent blue (for boys) & pink (for girls). I've got a black pair as spares to wear in sports lessons so that I don't break the 'proper' glasses my mother has forked out for. Think of them as stunt glasses. She is horrified when I start wearing the NHS specs full-time. But it's too late – Elvis has transformed them from a symbol of handicap/poverty into Pop Star Glasses.

So, my look is an amalgam of that of three lead singers. Prescient or what?

It's understandable that I tried to copy the image of musicians I admired at the time. Lots of people do it. It's called being a fan. You hope that a little of their creativity & talent might rub off on you too. Get you started.

Clothes & image are a good entry point. A statement of intent. But to move things further along I was going to have to do more. Put the theories into practice. Try myself out on the real world. I needed to locate MY creativity rather than try to borrow it from others.

In other words: I was going to have to start writing some songs.

Chapter Six

Creating something new is a
daunting prospect when you're
starting out.

You take a look at all the existing 'masterpieces', 'rock classics' & 'tour-de-forces' in the world & think, 'Who am I kidding? How can I ever compete with that?' It's easy to give up before you've even tried. Or you can get lost in displacement activity. Get the costumes together. Write the manifesto. Buy some cream laid paper. Sharpen some pencils. Get so wrapped up in the preparations that you lose sight of the job in hand.

It was a bit like that with this book. I talked about it a lot. Thought about going on a writer's retreat. Wondered what kind of pen I should use. In the end my editor gave me a strict deadline & told me to sit down & just write the thing. On a computer.

This Venus Perfect Pencils tin? I thought it would be good to store my Writer's Pen in. But it's still empty. COB.

How about these? Stylised brass figures representing a tortoise & a hare. They've got hefty spikes attached to the back of them & are connected by a short chain.

Is this brooch/fastener/piece of jewellery a keeper or a cobber? It intrigues me. It's the hare & tortoise thing. Which one are you? Are you a hare? Do you want things done 'yesterday'? Or are you a tortoise? Content to let events unfold at their own pace. Pausing for a rest every now & then.

I can state without hesitation that I'm on Team Tortoise. Sometimes that's a source of frustration for me. I wish I could be more prolific. I don't like the fact that it takes me so long to make a record or write a book or clear out a loft. But then I remember how Aesop's fable ends: the tortoise wins the race.

68

Love that idea.

I'm going to hang on to this for a little while longer. Who knows: maybe when this book comes out someone will get in touch & tell me what it is? KEEP.

Opposite, there's another page from the manifesto/exercise book. It's a graphic representation of how Pulp songs are going to revolutionise music as we know it.

Before Pulp: music is carrying on in much the same way as it has done for centuries.

After Pulp: the musical stave mutates into writhing, spaghetti-like forms completely new to mankind.

& just to hammer the point home I wrote some notes to go with the illustration:

'After having become well-known and loved by the nation's (and the world's) populace Pulp shall then proceed to widen the boundaries of contemporary music. By experimentation with new instruments and processes Pulp will attempt to nurture and develop new musical forms. Through their own efforts and their label-mates', they shall change the face of modern music.'

Pretty rich coming from someone who couldn't (& still can't) read a note of music.

The dream (as I think we've convincingly established by now) knew no bounds – but what was happening back on Planet Earth? What steps, if any, were being taken to make the dream a reality? These mythical songs weren't going to write themselves . . .

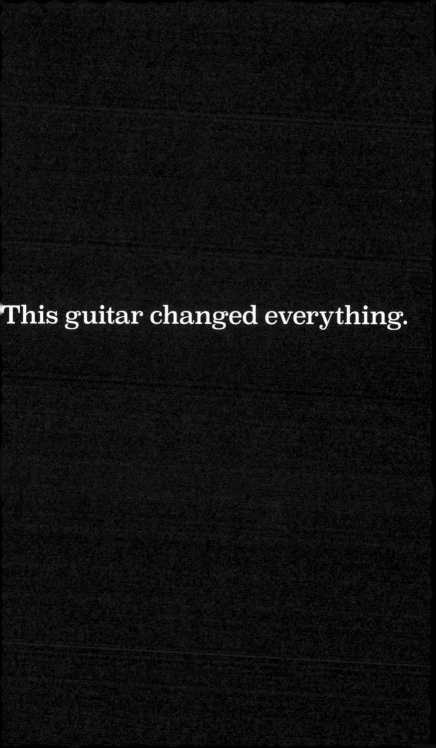

This guitar changed everything.

When punk came along & rendered my attempts to master the chords to 'Annie's Song' obsolete I was still trying to use the acoustic guitar that my mum had bought back in her art-school days. But punk bands didn't use acoustic guitars. Acoustic guitars were part of the old, square world punk had come to destroy. Punk wanted to drown out all that pretty, inconsequential strumming with the plugged-in, year-zero noise of electric guitars. I needed one.

Big problem. As we established earlier, I didn't have any money – & I was never going to find an electric guitar in a jumble sale.

The solution came from an unlikely source. Ibiza.

In the summer of 1976 I went on my first holiday abroad. My grandma & grandad decided to treat my mother, sister & I by taking us for a fortnight in the sun. Me & my sister were unimaginably excited. My sister is two years younger than me. She's called Saskia – another unusual name for the suburbs of Sheffield. Rembrandt's wife was called Saskia. My mum had heard the name during one of her art-history classes at college.

Back to the holiday. We'd never been on a plane before. Me & my sister took turns sitting in the window seat so that we could look at the clouds & the glimpses of the earth below. The aeroplane food came on a tray with everything in its own compartment, including a mini cruet set that we were told we could keep if we wanted (we did). Aeroplane food instantly became our favourite cuisine.

HOTELES
cartago
y galeon

Puerto San Miguel (IBIZA)

It was a package holiday. This is not a tale of Ibiza 'back in the day' – the roots of the counterculture, etc. We were in a large, modern hotel called Hotel Cartago, meals included. Every mealtime concluded with crème caramel as dessert. Sometimes the menu tried to disguise this by giving it different names. One night it was 'Cartago Pudding', the next 'Pudding of Two Tastes' (this involved the addition of chocolate sauce), another night it was 'Mystery Pudding' (no prizes for solving the mystery) & once even 'Orange Mousse' (a downright lie). 'Spot the Crème Caramel' became a family game to be played round the dinner table.

Another source of excitement was the fact that my sister & I had our own hotel room. This seemed incredibly sophisticated & luxurious. We were especially impressed by the walk-in wardrobe. 'You could sleep in there, it's so big,' we said in awed tones. Interesting idea . . .

One night we decided to do just that. We took a couple of pillows off the bed to make it more comfortable, pulled the slatted door shut from the inside & 'turned in'. The next thing I knew a torch was being shone in my face & all hell seemed to have broken loose. What was the problem? Well, my sister had been unable to sleep & so returned to the 'proper' bed. When my mum came in to check on us before she retired for the evening she saw one of the twin beds occupied & the other one empty – & panicked. A search party was sent out to look for a missing twelve-year-old English boy. With no results. My mum returned to our room, woke my sister & desperately asked if she knew where I'd gone. 'He's asleep in the wardrobe,' yawned Saskia. & I was.

For the rest of our stay I got funny looks from the hotel staff who had been involved in the night-time search for the strange kid who had a thing about sleeping in wardrobes. I didn't care – it was still Best Holiday Ever.

My mum enjoyed the holiday too: she got a new boyfriend. His name was Horst Hohenstein, he was German, & he taught people at the hotel how to scuba-dive. He drove around in an old armoured car that had been painted white, so of course me & Saskia thought he was great. He was also into music. Especially Pink Floyd. Pink Floyd wasn't 'radio' music. One song in particular got my attention: it sounded like it was being performed underwater & went on for ever. (I later found out it was 'Echoes' – the track that takes up the whole of Side 2 of *Meddle*.) Perfect music for a diving instructor to listen to. The armoured car had tiny windows with really thick glass in them in the rear compartment where my sister & I sat, so we pretended we were in a submarine, while Pink Floyd blared away in the background. Horst was fun.

He was the first adult I confessed my desire to be in a band to. He told me that he used to play bass in a band in his home town of Hamburg. I confided my secret longing to get hold of an electric guitar. He actually listened. He even seemed to think it was a good idea.

When it came to the end of the holiday, Horst drove us to Ibiza Airport in the armoured car. Before waving us off in the Departures Lounge he told me that he had spoken to my mother & he was going to come & spend Christmas with us in Sheffield. & he was going to bring something with him. An electric guitar. For me.

Chapter Seven

Before we go any further in the story of my musical development, I just want to show you this.

It's a battery-operated tin-plate model of the Apollo 11 Lunar Module. Before the arrival of the electric guitar this was the best Christmas present I'd ever received. The Moon landing took place on 20 August 1969 & I got it the following Christmas, which would make me six years old at the time. My space obsession goes back earlier than that though.

On the opposite page is a slide taken by my grandad two Christmases previously. Prise your eyes away from the rosy cheeks & 'interesting' socks & look at the object in the right-hand side of the photo. It looks out of place in an otherwise normal suburban front room, doesn't it? Is it a space rocket? A robot?

Close: it was made by my grandfather & it's his attempt at a Dalek. Doctor Who's journeys through space & time began on BBC Television in 1963, the year I was born. I was a fan. At the time I thought my grandad's recreation of the Doctor's nemesis was an exact replica. I thought the man was a genius. Now I can see it's not really that faithful to the original. It's still pretty impressive though – & it was interactive. The Dalek was mounted on castors & had a hinged door at the back so that I could get inside & trundle around the house shouting, 'Exterminate!' It was a very noisy Christmas that year.

Later, when I got too big to fit inside, I would push it unmanned into a room & shout, 'Exterminate!' from behind the door. Remote control. It ended up on a bonfire not long after that.

I mentioned earlier that the other dream career from my childhood was to be an astronaut & it's not hard to work out why. Space was everywhere when I was a kid. The dream space of TV shows like *Doctor Who* & *Star Trek* & the real space of the Apollo programme. As a child it was difficult to tell which was which.

countdown

ISSUE NO.   WEEK ENDING FEBRUARY 20, 1971 5p

DID FLYING SAUCERS EXIST ?

FREE
GIANT SPACEFACT
WALLCHART
with STAMPS ➜

THE BEST OF
TV SCIENCE FICTION

DOCTOR WHO

The secrets of **SHADO**

GERRY ANDERSON'S
THUNDERBIRDS
CAPTAIN SCARLET
*in ACTION-PACKED
PICTURE STORIES!*

UFO
FACT OR FICTION?

This comic had a lot to do with that confusion.

It's called *Countdown* & this is the very first issue (highly collectable). Doctor Who's there on the cover – but the main splash is 'UFO: FACT OR FICTION?' Good question. My other grandparents (on my father's side) lived next to a newsagent's & used to get me the comic every week. The pages are numbered backwards so that as you read your way through the comic you are getting nearer to blast-off. I took that literally.

It's set out like a cross between a comic book & a newspaper. You can see that on the double-page spread overleaf which has a *Thunderbirds* comic strip on one page & then a factual report on the development of the Space Shuttle on the other.

It gets even more confusing if you look a bit closer.

'SITUATIONS VACANT: Wanted, experienced astronaut, interesting assignments, must be willing to travel; an out-of-this-world opportunity.' Where do I apply? My young mind was boggled. The border line between fiction & reality fatally compromised. I became convinced that I was going to be spending my adult life in outer space. There was no reason for me to pay too much attention to earthbound things such as, say, learning to ride a bicycle – because who's going to be riding a bike in space? Preposterous idea. (I never owned a bicycle until I moved to London in 1988 – nearly twenty years later.)

Each week you got stickers free with the comic to put on the wall chart that came with the first issue. My wall chart has all the stickers on it (even more collectable). This wall chart was a campaign map for my upcoming life in space. There's a map of the Moon so you won't get lost among the craters. A map of the Milky Way for interstellar missions – 'bear left at Alpha Centauri & then head straight for 3 light years. You can't miss it.' You can even check out the vehicles you may be travelling in. 'I see you're looking at the Saturn 5, sir. Excellent choice. Fancy a test-drive?'

SO YOU WANT TO BE AN ASTRONAUT?

● SPACE SHUTTLE

New astronauts will be needed to man NASA's
Space Shuttle, the transportation system of the
future. Starting in 1977 the Shuttle will fly
once every two weeks, carrying cargo or
passengers to an orbiting space station. Both
the booster and the orbiter (which rides piggy-
back) have two-man crews. After separation,
the booster lands like an airliner, using
ordinary jet engines, and is re-used. The
orbiter completes its mission, then re-enters
and lands conventionally, also to be used again.
British Aircraft Corporation is doing design
studies for the Shuttle.

by our Space Correspondent

An astronaut of the 21st century may be
able to pick and choose his next job, but
today's spaceman undergoes years of rigorous
training to prepare for a single mission. More-
over, he spends only a few days of actual time
in space. James Lovell, commander of the
Apollo 12 moon mission, is a good example.
He has the most experience in space, yet in
his seven years as an astronaut he has spent
only 30 days in space. That means that between flights there are months and years of
training, studying and more training.

Where do astronauts come from? Many
are former jet pilots. The seven Mercury
astronauts were chosen in 1958 from over 100
pilots who had volunteered to give up their
flying careers for space training. Each of the
seven was a test pilot with 1,500 hours flying
time in jets. They were also qualified engineers
and in perfect physical condition. Other
astronauts have a scientific background,
specialising in geology or astrophysics, for
example.

During a one-week examination, teams of
doctors probe into the mind and body of each
trainee to make sure he is both mentally and
physically fit to pilot a spacecraft through
conditions varying from 8g to weightlessness.
Basic training for an American astronaut

lasts 18 months. And it starts in the classroom
—three days a week for the first four months,
the astronauts' school bell rings at 8 a.m. at
the Manned Spacecraft Centre in Houston,
Texas.

Each lesson lasts two hours; after two lecture periods the astronauts take a two-hour
break. But less than half of this is spent over
lunch. Before they sit down at the table the
men have a brisk work-out in the gym. Keeping in peak condition is essential, especially
while they are studying.

Half the instructors at the School for Astronauts are on the Houston staff. The other half
are experts from leading universities who are
brought in to lecture.

No astronaut gets to the top of his class,
because there is no grading. But tests are
carried out nearly every day.

Two days a week there's a break from
school. This gives the trainees a chance to
keep their jet-plane flying up to scratch or to
get acquainted with the workings of Mission
Control and have a look at the launch complex from which they will later blast off into
space.

*Next week in Part 2: the astronauts are
dropped by helicopter into a tropical jungle with
three days to find their way out.*

OUT IN THE BLACK VOID OF SPACE
ON THE EDGE OF A GREAT SPIRAL
GALAXY, A SLIGHT PIN-PRICK OF
LIGHT MOVES ALMOST IMPERCEPTIBLY
TOWARDS THE PLANET OF ITS ORIGIN
...EARTH!

THIS IS THE EARTH SHIP 'COUNTDOWN'... FOR FIFTY YEARS
THIS MAN-MADE COMPLEX HAS DRIFTED THROUGH THE
STARS TO HARVEST THE UNFATHOMABLE SECRETS OF THE
UNIVERSE AND FULFIL MANKIND'S AGE-OLD DREAM
AFTER A YEAR'S EXPLORATION OF THE STAR SYSTEM TAU
CETI, SHE IS NEARING JOURNEY'S END... LESS THAN
10,000 MILLION MILES SEPARATES HER FROM HOME...

SPACE INTRUDER DETECTOR, the eyes and ears of earth; detects and reports UFO activity, completing the three-pronged SHADO defences, including MOONBASE and SHADO control, in earth orbit, directly opposite the moon.

S.H.A.D.O.

SUPREME
HEADQUARTERS
ALIEN DEFENCE
ORGANISATION

MOONBASE

the fine pressurised domes is the Control Sphere.

Space Tracker (below) at the Control Sphere monitoring post.

The only earth-moon transport, earth ferry, makes a landing at MOONBASE.

SHADAIR

INTERCEPTORS

SHADO cars, 500 man-personal vehicles.

The SHADO jet fleet. Above, the flying lorry that carries the earth-moon ferry to the limit of the atmosphere.

SHADO MOBILES

Used by Straker, Foster and Freeman, special feature "gull-wing" doors for quick entry.

Shadair Transporter carries Mobiles to any site at Mach 1.

Supersonic passenger jet, equipped for automated landing.

SHADO CARS

MOBILES — all-purpose vehicle to investigate UFO landings in any terrain conditions.

Freeman, Straker, Foster, Shado riders, provide the secret ground support of SHADO Mobiles, Mobiles top speed: 50 mph (land), knots (water).

INTERCEPTORS, lunar strike power with computer-assisted missile; housed sub-surface in craters, to prevent UFO's from entering earth's atmosphere.

MOONMOBILE

MOONMOBILE (left), moon-based vehicle, lunar surface transport of men and equipment.

---

the PEOPLE... the MACHINES... that defend EAR

down at _____ 12   countdown at _____

---

countdown

ART: JOHN B[...]
SPACECRAFT D[...]
FROM THE MGM [...]
2001 : A SPAC[...]

SPACE AT [...]
[...]ND .

To complete your chart, collect picture stamps in the first six issues of Countdown, Space Age Comic.

Bell is a rocket-powered aircraft that set records with. Or a X-15 lander over California. After release it reached 4,000 mph, later scramjets went faster 9-10 plus.

[...]EM HAS
[...] ITS
[...]FLORA,

ON AND ON T[...]
CORRIDORS [...]
THE STERN [...]
BARRED BY A[...]

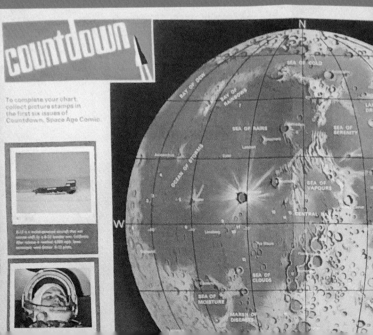

The final piece of the jigsaw, as far as I was concerned, was 'Countdown' – the strip that gave the comic its name – featuring 'SPACECRAFT DESIGNS FROM THE MGM FILM *2001: A SPACE ODYSSEY*'.

I went to see Stanley Kubrick's sci-fi masterpiece as a sixth birthday treat when it was re-released into UK cinemas in the wake of the real Moon landing that July. Fantasy & reality mixing again. I'd seen the poster for it during a shopping trip to Sheffield City Centre with my mum. It was showing at a cinema near the bus station called Cinecenta which, at the time, was the nearest Sheffield had to an arthouse cinema. My mother resisted my demands to go & see it because she said it would be 'too grown up' for me. But I was relentless & she finally gave in. Thus, on 19 September 1969, me & my friend from school John White (who was probably only there for the visit to the ice-cream parlour afterwards, to tell the truth) had our minds well & truly blown.

What can I add to the literature surrounding *2001: A Space Odyssey*? It's untouchable.

There are certain works of art that you encounter in the course of your lifetime that enlarge your perception of the world. They're the important ones. The ones that stay with you. *2001* didn't just enlarge my perception of the world: it introduced me to the whole cosmos! From the dawn of mankind to the outer reaches of the galaxy – with a ten-minute-long abstract, hallucinatory 'Stargate' sequence thrown in for good measure. Of course I didn't understand it. My mum was right: it *was* too grown up for me. Too big. Too long. Too deep. Too complex. Too . . . everything. But I loved it. & it's stayed with me ever since. I believed it. I believed life was going to be an adventure on an epic scale that no one could really understand. Conducted somewhere out in Deep Space. 'To infinity & beyond' as someone said a few (light) years later. There was no way back.

I was in the right place at the right time. A week later & I might have been profoundly transformed by *The Italian Job*. Imagine that.

My mum must have been impressed too because she bought the 2001 soundtrack album. She sometimes hosted Tupperware parties & would put it on during the 'socialising' section of the evening. It's a great soundtrack – but it's certainly not a party record. Those long, wordless vocal pieces by György Ligeti were the scariest music I ever heard coming up through the floorboards of my childhood bedroom. It was like there was a satanic mass happening down in the living room rather than an innocent Tupperware party.

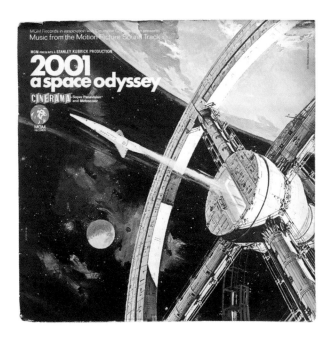

Here I am in that selfsame living room. This is a very rare picture of the battery-operated Apollo 11 American Eagle Lunar Module in action. I am looking a little underwhelmed in this photo because I've just realised that you can't really 'play' with this toy. Once you have flicked the 'on' switch it rushes furiously around on the carpet of its own volition with its 'lunar antenna' spinning really quickly, making a hell of a racket. The most interesting thing it does is to pause occasionally & lower a ramp with a silver spaceman on it. My sister looks to be enjoying herself much more than I am. That's because she's about to place a green Smartie on the spaceman's ramp the next time it lowers so that he's 'got something to eat'. When the ramp goes back up again & the module resumes its demented dance across the floor the Smartie will fall inside the toy & melt & cause the motor to short-circuit. Whereupon the lunar module will grind to a halt, never to move again from that day to this.

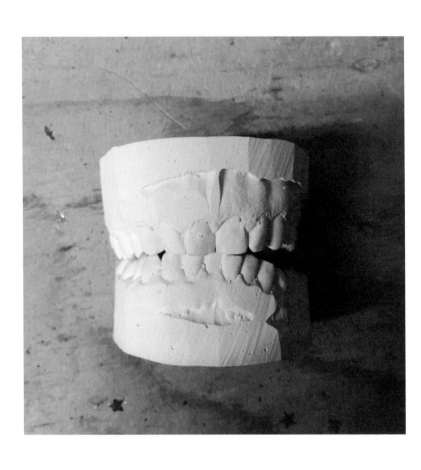

Chapter Eight

I think we've got our teeth into this now. We're uncovering some pivotal objects & getting to the roots of some obsessions/ inspirations.
(Is there really any difference between the two?)

I just hope we haven't bitten off more than we can chew . . .

These are my teeth – or rather, a plaster-cast of my teeth. I had a lot of work done on them when I was a kid. I was told I had two teeth too many in the upper jaw & they would have to come out & then I would need to wear a brace for quite a while. Believe it or not, this is the 'after' cast.

The first dentist to rise to the challenge of fixing my smile was Dr Tinker, whose practice was between our home & school. Dr Tinker had lost an eye in the war & wore a patch over the wound. To say it gave him a sinister aspect would be an understatement. All kids are scared stiff of going to the dentist to begin with but the patch took this dread to a whole new level. 'Gas & air' being the anaesthetic of choice in those days, Dr Tinker would place the breathing apparatus over your mouth & nose & then ask you to count to ten out loud. Around number seven, when everything was starting to go grainy & sibilant, he would come over to remove the breathing mask & begin his work. The last image in your tender, young mind, as unconsciousness loomed & he bent over you, drill in hand, was Dr Tinker's eye patch flapping open to reveal the horror of what lay beneath. 'Is it safe?'

After a number of the fillings that Dr Tinker had inserted proved to be 'unsafe' (they fell out) – I started going to another dentist a little further afield. Dr Khalsi was a Sikh, wore a turban & was altogether more pleasant than his predecessor. The rest of my 'oral refurb' went without a hitch. This cast must have been made by Dr Khalsi in celebration of the end of his treatment. I used to have it displayed on the bookshelf in my bedroom with some little plastic legs from an Airfix kit poking out between the incisors. A trophy from my years in the Tooth Wars.

I read in a Dream Dictionary once that a dream about losing one's teeth symbolises a fear of loss of sexual potency, so let's put this cast somewhere safe, eh? KEEP.

Ceasefire was declared in the Tooth Wars just before Christmas 1976.

True to his word, Horst Hohenstein arrived at our family home on Christmas Eve. Me & my sister ran out to meet him in the yard in front of the house. He was carrying one large silvery metal trunk. No sign of a guitar. I prepared myself for a disappointment. I had history with this sort of thing.

I told you that my father left home when I was seven years old. What I didn't tell you was that he then emigrated to Australia. So there was none of that 'McDonald's handover' business (McDonald's didn't open a branch in Sheffield until 1985 anyway, but you get what I mean) – no dual households. He simply disappeared from our lives overnight. I did get birthday cards from him though. With a handwritten message inside that invariably finished with the words, 'I've put your present in the post.' You can probably guess how this story ends. Suffice to say there were many fruitless vigils awaiting the arrival of the postman in the morning.

So when I saw Horst lugging that metal trunk into the house with no guitar case in sight I prepared myself for a similar experience. Though the trunk was large it wasn't long enough to fit a guitar inside. He'd probably forgotten. That's what adults did.

But I was in for a pleasant surprise.

I guess he must have picked up on my mood because he opened the trunk the minute he got in the house & there was . . . half a guitar.

It was just the body of a guitar with no neck. Dismembered. It turned out he'd only been allowed one item of luggage on his flight & had dismantled the guitar so he could keep his promise to me. In another part of the trunk, the neck was wrapped up in some of his clothes. He asked my mum for a screwdriver & began to put the two back together. After that he re-strung the guitar & handed it over to me. & life was never the same again.

The guitar was made in Germany by a company called Hopf. It's not a revered or collectable brand. It's got 'f-holes',

like a cello or a violin, making it a 'semi-acoustic' guitar. Did that make it only semi-electric or semi-punk as well? Up till now I'd been dealing only with the 'idea' of an electric guitar & how it could help me realise my ambition of becoming a pop star. It was a wish-fulfilment totem like the McCulloch hair, the Cornwell beard & the Costello specs. Now it was here in our kitchen.

What was I going to do with it? How did I hold it? How did I tune it?

I have a friend who likes to tell the story of how, when he got his first electric guitar, he tried to fit a 13-amp plug to the end of the jack-to-jack cable that came with it. He thought an electric guitar was like an electric toaster or an electric kettle & had to be plugged into the mains. Luckily his dad intervened before he connected it to the wall socket. That would have been a very short career in music.

I wasn't quite that clueless – but not that far off either. Horst informed me the guitar sounded much better through an amplifier than played acoustically. Luckily, I had anticipated this scenario & had badgered my grandma & grandad into buying me a serious bit of technology for Christmas.

It's in here somewhere . . .

After Recording System

FULL AUTO SHUT OFF

COUNTER

0 0 0

HEAD PHONE   OUTPUT

 TENSAI RHYTHM MACHINE

(Guitaraok

FULL AUTO SHUT OFF

SLOW ROCK | ROCK BEAT

TAPE | RADIO | RHYTHM

FUNCTION SELECT

anyone?)

This is no ordinary cassette recorder: it has an input so you can play a guitar through it. It also has a switch so that you can record yourself & then play back that recording & add something else on top. Multi-track recording.

It's even got a drum machine built into it so you can also tape yourself playing along to a rhythm track. &, as if that wasn't enough, you can also record yourself playing along to songs on the radio if you want. (Guitaraoke, anyone?) It's a versatile machine.

Unfortunately, the cassette mechanism is broken so I can't demonstrate all these features to you. Couldn't bring myself to throw it away though. (I guess that comes as no surprise to you by now.) This contraption, combined with the Hopf guitar, comprised my entire after-school life for the next three years.

No more hanging out on the street corner with the other kids. I would come home, watch TV, eat my tea & then go to my bedroom & play. My mother called it 'plinky-plonking' (she still does sometimes).

Now, there are more embarrassing things a teenage boy can get up to in his bedroom on his own, I guess . . . but the idea that my mother, & to a lesser extent my sister, could hear what I was doing up there was a problem for me. Finding an idea is messy. Very messy. & I had no formal training. I was making it up as I went along. Casting around in a state of nervous tension, hoping to come up with something that sounded . . . like me.

My 'process' hasn't really changed that much in the intervening years. I still have to 'gee myself up' – get 'in the zone' or however you want to describe it – when I'm trying to write something new. I'll typically plug in a guitar or a keyboard & turn it up quite loud so that I have to make an effort to be heard singing over it. That's important: I'm hoping the noise will dislodge something inside me. An unexpected emotion or viewpoint. The struggle to make my voice audible seems to help with that. But this combination of high-volume, untutored musical experimentation, plus emotionally invested yelping can sound pretty freaky. Passers-by might think some kind of Guantánamo Bay-style torture scenario is going on.

So the thought that my mum & sister downstairs could hear this hit-&-miss process was mortifying to me back then. Especially because I was just starting out.

I was trying to find my own voice without being overheard. Pretty impossible.

Looking back, it's probably no coincidence that my attempts to play music coincided with going through puberty. I hadn't *thought* sex into my life. It came of its own accord (behave). It was like it had been hidden inside my body all along waiting for the cue to move centre-stage.

The first clues that something was going on in that area had been the appearance of pubic hair. My sister caught me inspecting it one day & ran out of the room laughing hysterically & told my mum. Up to that point we had shared a bedroom – me on the top bunk & her below. Now she was banished to the spare room & the bunk beds were dismantled & replaced by an old double bed from my grandparents' house next door.

If something as powerful as the sex instinct had been lurking undiscovered inside me for years & years, who knew what other things might be floating around down there as well? They might even turn out to be as pleasurable. Playing the guitar & attempting to write songs were a way of finding out. A song is an adventure you go on inside yourself. By strumming away alone in my bedroom I was dropping a line down into the murky depths, hoping for a bite. Hoping to take myself by surprise. Gone fishin'.

Too much musical self-exploration could get tiring though. Plus, my mum & sister might be trying to watch something on TV downstairs during my 'expeditions'. As soon as someone shouted upstairs for me to 'turn that noise down' the spell was broken. No problem: at the flick of a switch the In Tensai Rhythm Machine could change from '2 Track' mode (playing guitar, yelping along & recording the results) to 'Normal' mode (ready to record from the radio). This was the other way in which this cassette recorder dominated my teenage years. From Monday to Thursday, between 10 p.m. & midnight, I lay in my double bed listening to the John Peel radio show on BBC Radio 1, poised to record any music that caught my fancy. Another kind of 'fishing'.

For the thirty-seven years John Peel was broadcasting at the BBC he was the only outlet for alternative music on British radio. There is no way to quantify that. Without his show so much of the music we have been brought up with, & take for granted, simply would not exist.

I discovered him by accident.

When punk broke it was easier to read about than to listen to. After the Sex Pistols appeared on the Bill Grundy show & swore on live TV it was all over the papers – 'The Filth & the Fury', etc. – but nowhere to be heard on the radio. Many radio stations actively took a stand against it. They thought it was a threat to the moral fibre of the nation (sounds quaint now, doesn't it? that music could be considered that 'dangerous').

One such station was Radio Hallam, Sheffield's commercial radio broadcaster. I remember hearing Colin Slade, the presenter of the *Hallam Rock* show, reassure his listeners that he wouldn't be playing any punk rock on his programme because it wasn't 'real music'. Of course, that made me all the more determined to hear some. I went over to the radio & started turning the tuning knob.

I was almost all the way to the end of the dial when I stopped. There was a guy singing in a strange, high, whiny voice. The music in the background wasn't loud & aggressive, as I imagined punk to be, but the overall effect was . . . different. I took my hand off the tuner & listened. When the song ended a deeper voice (one I was to become very familiar with) informed me that I had just been listening to Elvis Costello. On the *John Peel Show*. My musical education had entered its next phase.

My favourite hobby now became making tape compilations of songs that I heard on his programme. The music was so different to the chart pop I'd been reared on. I did find the punk that I'd been searching for – but I found much more too. Reggae, noise, experimental, modern classical – a whole new world of music.

An example: on my fourteenth birthday (19 September 1977) the show featured the first radio session by The Slits. The Slits were an all-female band. They didn't have a record deal when they recorded the session for the show. One song was called 'Shoplifting' & it was only about a minute long & actually sounded like they were doing some shoplifting in the middle of it. One member of the band shouted, 'Do a runner!' while the rest of them screamed. The music was quite haphazard & sounded like it was constantly on the verge of collapse. This was encouraging. Usually when I compared ideas I'd recorded on the Rhythm Machine against songs taped off the radio I was dismayed by the yawning chasm that existed between the two. I was still so far off sounding 'proper'. But The Slits' session didn't sound that distant. It was rough – but in a good way. & it sounded more alive than anything else Peel played that night. It reinforced the idea that songs were about more than mere musicianship. Musicianship had led rock music down a blind alley. 'Shoplifting' showed an escape route. I was absolutely ready to do a runner.

The sounds I was capable of making didn't sound 'professional' but they were *my* sounds. & in the end that was more important than being in tune or in time or other boring details like that. There was hope for me.

Whenever I'm asked 'What is your greatest musical influence?' My reply is, 'John Peel'. Those years spent lying in the dark listening to his show with the radio cassette recorder right next to the bed, so that I could still hear it properly at low volume & therefore avoid being told off because I had school in the morning, were invaluable. They were my real education.

& the outpouring of tributes after John Peel's death in 2004 bear testament to the fact that I was most definitely not the only person he performed this service for. In his quiet, unassuming way he'd been expanding music lovers' horizons for nigh on forty years.

CATHEDRAL OF ST. JAMES
BURY ST EDMUNDS

John R.P. Ravenscroft
1939 - 2004

Friday 12th November 2004
1.00pm

Chapter Nine

This is the remains of a bar of
Cussons Imperial Leather soap.

To be exact, it is the label of a bar of Cussons Imperial Leather soap with a very small amount of the actual soap left attached to it. I'm not in the habit of washing myself in storage spaces: this is in the loft because Cusson's changed the Imperial Leather label design some time in the mid '90s & this upset me greatly. This is what's left of the last bar of soap that I could find with the original label. That made it precious. I remember going to a lot of supermarkets trying to find Imperial Leather in its old packaging when the changeover began. A lot of groping to the back of dusty shelves. Eventually the new bar was everywhere. I used this bar of soap for as long as was humanly possible & then couldn't bring myself to throw it away when it became more label than soap. So here it is.

The Imperial Leather adverts on TV when I was a child depicted an opulent lifestyle. I remember one featuring a family on the Trans-Siberian Express travelling in a carriage that had a sunken bath. It was luxury in soap form.

The only people I knew who used Imperial Leather were my dad's parents. Saskia & I used to go & stay with them sometimes. They ran a post office & lived in the flat above it. Definitely *not* an opulent lifestyle. Their flat backed on to a railway line & I would wash my hands before bed, looking out through the frosted glass of the bathroom window at the blurry lights of passing trains. The smell of the soap combined with the noise of the trains on the tracks produced quite a sensory trip. Sometimes I would enhance the experience by turning the hot tap very slightly to the 'on' position, which did something strange to the pressure in the water system, causing the pipes to honk & judder in a violent fashion. It sounded like a goose was being tortured in the airing cupboard. I loved it. This Peak Experience never lasted long though, as my grandma would rush in & tell me I was going to cause a burst pipe. But I had caught a glimpse of paradise . . .

I have had this remnant of a bar of soap for a quarter of a century now. So when I first found it in the loft I thought to myself, 'Could it be time to let this go? Could this be a chance to finally move on? It's just a piece of horrible old dried-up soap, after all . . .' Get real.

But, as you can see, I haven't thrown it away.

I've kept it because it reminds me of a major character trait I have grappled with throughout my life: a profound aversion to change.

I can say this with authority because there are other examples that bear witness to this behaviour.

Exhibit B: Marmite jars used to have yellow tin lids featuring a red stripe across them with 'Marmite' printed on it. They phased out the metal lid in the mid '80s & replaced it with a plain yellow plastic one which has endured to the present day. Similar story: I kept hold of one of the metal lids & whenever I bought a new jar of Marmite I would remove the plastic lid, throw it in the bin, & replace it with the metal one. This went on for about a year until someone else in the shared house I was living in finished off the Marmite & then threw away both jar & lid without my knowledge. That was a bad day. 'Aha,' I hear you cry, 'so what's it doing in here if it got thrown away?' OK – you got me bang to rights: I found this jar in a junk shop some years later & couldn't resist buying it. Breaking these habits takes some time. Everyone is entitled to a relapse now & then. Cut me some slack.

Old   New

Exhibit C: More recently, 'Rose's Lime Juice' changed their label & bottle design. (May even have happened during the present century.) This was when I realised I might have a problem with this kind of behaviour. Cussons Imperial Leather soap was connected to a cherished childhood experience. Marmite was a product I had detested as a kid but had got heavily into once past adolescence. Rose's Lime Juice, however, wasn't something I even remotely liked. My only contact with it was seeing it displayed on supermarket shelves or in my grandma's kitchen cupboard. But as soon as I saw the new design in the local corner shop I went & bought a bottle of the old type anyway. & then it stood on the work surface near the cooker getting dusty because I really didn't like the taste. Far too sharp. I had bought it simply because I saw the design was changing & not because it had any personal resonance.

Time to stage an 'intervention'. I threw the bottle of lime cordial away. The photos opposite were not taken by me. Perhaps they are the work of another 'change denier'. Perhaps there is a support group for this condition. Personally, I now feel I have escaped this phobia of change. At least, I hope I have. It was the Rose's Lime Juice that did it. It brought it to my attention. One day at a time though . . .

Finding the Cusson's Imperial Leather soap fragment a couple of years ago was another one of the starting points for this book. For twenty-five years it had been adrift in this dark loft space, just part of the swamp. I couldn't derive any pleasure from it because it wasn't available to me. It's now a conversation piece, proudly exhibited. Look, it's even got its own display case.

Once I put it on display I realised that, rather than being a source of shame & irritation, this loft could do something positive for me. Could help me come to terms with certain aspects of my personality.

Why am I mistrustful of change? Am I a hoarder? What am I trying to hide? These are important questions. Not every object we unearth is going to end up in such an exalted position (there's even been a film made about this piece of soap!) but they all count. Because they're all here. They all happened. They're the undisputed truth.

The truth to be gleaned from the Imperial Leather soap fragment is (I hope): I am 'over' my problem with change. I embrace change. (Maybe 'embrace' is too strong a word: more like I 'awkwardly shake hands' with change.) I can move on.

& anyway:

Look what I found when I was helping my mother move house recently. Original design. Bath size. Box unopened. Still sealed.

Just for old times' sake.

Chapter Ten

There are a lot of pairs of broken glasses up here in the loft. That's not because I'm always getting into punch-ups.

In fact, I've only had one fist fight in my entire life. It was at Junior School. We were playing football in the school yard during the dinner break & I was the goalie. We were playing the 'jumpers for goalposts' version of the game. A kid called Peter Cook had a shot & he said it went in & I said it didn't & neither of us would back down until, out of the blue, he said, 'Wanna fight?' The other kids in the yard gathered round us & started chanting, 'Fight! Fight!' (In their South Yorkshire accents it sounded more like 'Feet! Feet!') & I got carried away by the sense of occasion & replied, 'Yeah.' At that very moment the bell to mark the end of break rang. But I was not saved by the bell – hasty arrangements were made for the fight to take place on the school field when home time came around.

The rest of the school day was horrendous. I couldn't concentrate. I got a sickening, lurching feeling every time I remembered what was in store once school finished. If the fight had just happened there & then in the heat of the moment it probably would have been over in a matter of seconds. & then forgotten about. This drawn-out anticipation made it so much worse.

The really crazy bit about it was that we were friends. The fact we both wore glasses had been a source of bonding between us. & now we were going to have a fight! I think that's why the other kids in the school yard had been so eager to fan the flames of our flare-up. They wanted to see what a fight between two 'four-eyed gets' looked like. An exotic treat.

The school bell rang. Seconds out, Round 1 . . .

As we walked to the school field I could tell that Peter had gone off the idea too – but neither of us could bring ourselves to back out & risk being called 'chicken'.

friends at ....City...School............7.6..........

Name M.e. (alias Spider-man)
Address ...130. Mansfield
Rd...Sheffield. 12.....

Name Cookeo. (alias.Peter
Address ....
....

We reached the football pitch & the spectators formed a ring around us. We each gave our glasses to someone to hold. The self-appointed referee told us that 'first one to cry is the loser'. We nodded our assent. & the longest fight in Intake Junior School's history began.

Maybe it was because we were friends. Maybe it was because neither of us had been in a fight before. Maybe it was because we couldn't really see each other without our glasses. For my part, I found it absolutely impossible to punch Peter in the face. You see that kind of thing on TV all the time but in real life it felt so . . . wrong. Impossibly brutal. So I went for rapid body punches. I must have seen a boxer do that to a punchbag on some sports programme. A lot of the 'fight' was us circling each other whilst the crowd bayed for blood. Then we would rush together & make contact. Peter didn't seem to want to punch me in the face either. So it turned into more of a wrestling contest. He wrestled me to the ground at one point & I remember seeing my hand all pale & mottled-looking against the green of the football pitch while he pummelled my back. The 'ref' kept asking if either of us wanted to 'submit'. He'd obviously got that phrase from watching wrestling on ITV on Saturday mornings. Mick McManus & Catweazle & those other strange characters in costume. 'Two falls or a submission' & all that.

In the end the audience submitted before we did. People started drifting off because they didn't want to be late for their tea. Philistines. In a final flurry of shame & humiliation Peter & I came together & I ended up with a black eye & he got a cauliflower ear. Neither of us cried though. The fight was declared a draw (another first in the history of the school).

I did my crying on the way home. The small-scale experience of blood lust sickened me. & how you could be bullied into doing something by peer pressure.

Now that I'd experienced a fight first-hand I vowed never to have one again. & I haven't. (As far as I know, our school-fight duration record still stands.)

So, these glasses didn't get broken due to me being in fights. The reason there are so many pairs of broken spectacles up here is that they have been trodden on. By me.

I am severely short-sighted so I have to be careful where I put my glasses when I go to bed at night. When I was living in more precarious circumstances this was an issue because my bed would invariably be a mattress on the floor. If I didn't pay adequate attention to where I'd put my glasses for any reason (drink/extreme fatigue/sex) then I was playing a game of Russian Roulette when I woke up. After a period of squinting intensely into the twilight of the bedroom, I would hop around in an uncomfortable crouching position hoping to see the dim glint of a lens. There would eventually come a sickening crunch from underfoot. Oh, there you are . . .

Such a shitty way to start the day. Often, I would just go straight back to bed.

There's a lot of stuff here in the loft that could easily get trampled underfoot & broken. Like this little guy, for instance. But be careful – he's priceless: for years he has been the sole reminder of the reason I wear glasses in the first place.

When I was six years old I caught meningitis. Meningitis is an infection of the protective membrane that surrounds the brain & spinal cord. It can be deadly if it's not treated quickly enough. I complained of pains in my legs after a family visit to the swimming baths. The pains didn't go away & worsened after I'd gone to bed. My mum got worried & phoned our family GP, Mrs Fantham, who recognised the symptoms & told my mother to get me to hospital immediately. I don't remember much about that because the disease begins to cause delirium & paralysis due to pressure on the brain. The next thing I do remember is being told to curl up in the foetal position by a doctor because he was going to perform a lumbar puncture. I had no idea what that meant but the 'puncture' bit didn't sound good. When I saw the syringe he was going to 'puncture' me with I knew for sure it wasn't good. It was so big it looked like a comedy syringe from a cartoon. The needle was five inches long. Imagine how threatening that would look to a six-year-old child. Especially when accompanied by the words, 'This is going to be very painful but if you're a good boy, & you don't cry, you can see your mum after.' I promised not to cry.

The Wikipedia entry on 'lumbar puncture' (or a 'spinal tap' as it is known in the US) reads, 'A spinal needle is inserted between the lumbar vertebrae & pushed in until there is a "give" as it enters the lumbar cistern. The needle is again pushed until there is a second "give" that indicates the needle is past the dura mater.' In layman's terms that means a humungous needle is pushed through your backbone into your spinal column. Twice. The pain was unbelievable. But I didn't cry.

'Can I see my mum now?' I whimpered after the needle was removed.

'She's gone home,' came the reply. Sensitive. She obviously hadn't been there earlier when he made me promise not to cry. As we established earlier: adults lie.

I was in an isolation ward at the Sheffield Children's Hospital. I received lots of hand-drawn cards from my classmates at school. Our teacher must have written something on the blackboard for the class to copy because they all had the same message inside them. Perhaps Sheffield Education Board had a standard 'words to write in the event of a pupil contracting a life-threatening illness' letter.

(See overleaf.)

Intake country School
Thursday July 24
Dear Jarvis we hope you
will be better soon we have
been busy at school getting
ready for the summer
holidays

Love from
Gail Perkins

Intake country School
Thursday July 24th Dear Jarvis
we hope you
will be better soon
we have been getting
ready for the summer
holidays Love from victoria

Intake country School
Thursday July 24th
Dear Jarvis we
hope you will be
better soon
we have been
busy at school
getting ready
for the summer
holidays. Love
from Philip Wilson

Intake county School
Thursday July 24th
Dear Jarvis
we hope you
will be better
soon We have been
busy at school
getting ready for
the summer
holiday Love from Louise

Intake county School
Thursday July 24th
Dear Jarvis
we hope you
will be better
soon we have been
busy at school
getting ready for
the summer holidays
Love from Mandy

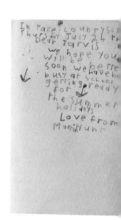

Intake country School
Thursday July 24 th
Dear Jarvis
we hope you
will be better
soon we have
busy at school
getting ready
for
the summer
holidays
Love from
Mandy Hunt

I also received lots of great presents. People must really have thought I was about to snuff it. But I didn't. The illness gradually subsided &, after two weeks or so, I was told I would be going home the next day. Then came the bombshell: due to the fact that they might be infected with the virus I'd just had, all the fantastic gifts I'd been given would have to be incinerated. All of them.

All except this guy. A relative who was aware of my space obsession had bought me some plastic spacemen to play with. They were the most 'cheap tack' present I'd received. Must have cost about 20p from the corner shop. But the spacemen survived precisely due to their poor quality: because they were made out of plastic they could be sterilised in boiling water. Which meant they could come home with me. & here's the last member of the mission still in my possession – the Last Astronaut Standing, if you will.

Most people don't escape a case of meningitis scot-free. There are a variety of after-effects. Damaged eyesight is one of the most common. I've worn glasses ever since.

This is the story that I've told myself (& anyone else that was interested) throughout my entire life. It's a touching story. An almost heroic story. & it's all true. All except for one very important detail.

That's not why I wear glasses.

Oh look, here's Marianne Faithfull's first album, released in April 1965. I didn't hear it until Christmas 1985 when I was given it as a present by my girlfriend of the time. I say 'girlfriend of the time': we were in the death throes of the relationship – that stage when you split up, then get back together, only to split up once again. It looks very cold written down like that. But this was my first long-term relationship & the fact that it had gone wrong was really painful. For both of us. & we lacked the emotional vocabulary to deal with it.

For instance, splitting up around Christmas is really crap. You're surrounded by this 'Peace & Goodwill to all men' business, which makes dumping someone seem really mean. Like you're the Scrooge of the romance scene. So we'd bought each other presents. We didn't know any better.

When I put this record on that Christmas it destroyed me. The first track is called 'Come & Stay With Me'. Cards on the table from the off.

Then comes 'If I Never Get to Love You' which begins:

> If I never get to love you,
> It won't be that I didn't try.
> I'll be trying to possess you
> 'Til the day I die.

Another pretty stark message. The album was littered with them. Other track titles include: 'He'll Come Back to Me', 'In My Time of Sorrow', 'What Have I Done Wrong?', 'I'm a Loser' – by the end of Side 2 I was an emotional wreck. My girlfriend was eviscerating me by way of these songs delivered in Marianne's pure, innocent voice. O, Come All Ye Faithfull. I was not 'of good cheer' that festive season.

Another year, another festive season, just before Christmas 2012, Pulp played a home-town concert in Sheffield. It was the finale of a reunion tour which had healed some old rifts & settled some scores. There is a film by Florian Habicht called *Pulp: A Story About Life, Death & Supermarkets* which is based around the show we did that night. In an interview featured in the film I describe my motivation for being involved in the Pulp reunion as a desire to 'tidy up' in some way. I thought the way the group had ended was 'messy'. (There is obviously a precedent for the process we are going through here in the loft. I have history with this kind of behaviour.) At the post-concert party I was surprised to bump into my first girlfriend. The one who had given me the Marianne Faithfull album. In honour of the 'healing' spirit in which the tour had been undertaken I told her how sorry I was for the way things had ended between us & how moved I'd been by the way she'd tried to communicate her pain to me through the gift she gave me that Christmas over a quarter of a century ago. She looked at me & smirked. 'I bought that Marianne Faithfull record because it was on offer at WHSmith & I didn't want to spend too much on your present because I knew you were going to pack me. I never listened to it.'

We tell ourselves stories based on evidence we glean from the world. We arrange that information in what appears to be a logical order & it becomes a narrative we believe in. It becomes

The Truth. These truths can endure for years & years. Often for a whole lifetime. But, every now & then, something happens to make us reconsider them.

My mum was ill a couple of years ago & I went to look after her whilst she was convalescing at home. Going back into that parent/child dynamic years after you've flown the nest is quite something. It's hard to avoid falling into old patterns of behaviour. I wasn't walking around the house in lederhosen or anything like that, but you get the picture. Ornaments on shelves, books in the bookcase, objects that used to surround me on a daily basis made the distance between the past & the present feel wafer-thin. We fell into reminiscing on our family history at mealtimes. Usually I do pretty badly in these discussions because my mum will launch into some story about Uncle Branson or Aunty Sailie & I haven't got a clue who she's talking about. Then she gets irritated with me & says, 'You must remember!' & gives a detailed physical description of the person in question, which still doesn't help. It's a joke in our family that I have no recollection at all of important life events & yet can tell you who drew the first *Spider-Man* comics (Steve Ditko followed by John Romita) or the actors that played Batman & Robin in the original 1960s TV series (Adam West & Burt Ward). Further examples of what a grip pop had on me as a kid.

On one particular evening I was trying to get in the Family Chronicles spirit by coming up with some reminiscences of my own. I asked how long it had been after I was discharged from hospital that the school realised my eyesight had been affected & recommended that I go to the optician's for an eye test.

'What are you on about?' came the reply. 'You were wearing glasses before you went to hospital.'

'Are you sure?' She'd just had quite a serious illness so maybe she was still a bit confused.

'Course I'm sure,' she said, 'I can prove it.' & with that she laboriously manoeuvred herself out of her chair & came back a few minutes later with a photograph.

It looks innocent enough – here I am proudly showing off my Sheffield Wednesday football kit. Surrounded by all the books & nick-nacks my mum has held on to. But behind me is a row of cards. Birthday cards. I'm showing off the football kit because it's a present I've just received for my sixth birthday. I'm wearing my favourite present – & I'm also quite clearly wearing glasses. & I wasn't admitted to hospital with meningitis until two months after this picture was taken.

It's strange to discover that a story you've told yourself for almost your entire life turns out to be completely false. Especially when it's one you're involved in. If *you* don't know your own life story then who does?

As my mum told it, my myopia was discovered soon after I started school at the age of five. I couldn't see a thing that the teacher wrote or drew on the blackboard. I was moved to the front row of desks but I still had problems. I was duly sent home with a note for my mother. She looked sheepish as she related the next part of the story. 'We didn't know,' she said. 'You never said anything or complained. I suppose your eyes must have been as bad as that since the day you were born.'

Hold on a minute! I have just got up from my computer & gone to find a tape measure. If I take my glasses off & hold my hand in front of my face I can keep it in focus up to a distance of about 9 inches. Everything beyond that is a total blur. My optical prescription hasn't changed that much in the years since I first started wearing glasses. Maybe a centimetre or so. That means I spent the first five years of my life LIVING IN A FOG!

I'd heard the story about having to move to the front of the class because I couldn't see what was on the blackboard. & I'd also heard the story about how, when I came out of the optician's wearing my first pair of glasses, I'd looked up & said, 'Oh, there are holes in the trees!' Meaning that up till that point trees had just been green blobs to me & now I could see patches of sky through gaps in the leaves. These were parts of the Family Chronicle that I was familiar with. I'd just got the chronology wrong. I'd placed those events after my return home from hospital following my bout of meningitis when constructing my own personal timeline.

How do I adjust to the revelation of The Fog Era? There's a sense of disappointment when something you hold to be true is disproved. It's like me trying to hold on to my Primal Wogan even in the face of *Blankety Blank* Wogan. I thought mine was better. Do I really have to face up to reality?

It's obvious that spending the first five years of my life in a soft-focus haze cannot help but have had a profound effect on my development – but I DON'T REMEMBER ANY OF IT.

I can make guesses. Is that why there are so many plastic novelties up here that look like they could have come out of a Christmas cracker? Because they would have been the only playthings the young me could see in their entirety? Is that why I started reading at such an early age? Because books could be held within my shallow 'depth-of-field'? Is that why I love music so much? Because you don't have to worry whether it's in 'focus' or not – my ears could pick it up no problem? Is that why I've had this lifelong obsession with details & minutiae in all the work I've done? Because at one time that was ALL I COULD SEE? My entire existence would have consisted of details – the rest of the world just fuzzy vagueness. I would have had no idea or real inkling of the Bigger Picture.

There's no way of knowing the full extent of the effect of The Fog Era. But five years *is* a long time. Especially when those five years happen to be the first five years of your life. The Fog had profound effects.

Although The Fog has not entirely lifted, I've learnt to live with it over the years. I now take precautions (see above). I took this photo when I was staying at a friend's recently & there was no bedside table in the room I was sleeping in. Why take chances? I enjoy The Fog now. I like waking up in the warm, fuzzy gloom & being able to make the decision as to exactly when I want the world to snap into focus. Take the glasses down off the hanger & pass from one mode of existence to another. Not everyone can do that.

In the first part of this book I have tried to detail some of the formative experiences that have led to me seeing the world in my own particular way. The ingredients that have created My Vision. Your ingredients will be different to mine but I do believe the basic recipe is the same for all of us.

It's now time to try ourselves out on some other people.

Interlude

THE MAGIC CIRCLE

I have worried about writing this book. Investigating the foundations of my creative life could bring the whole edifice crashing down about my ears.

Think of being a songwriter as like being a magician. If a magician divulges the methods behind his or her tricks they get thrown out of the Magic Circle. Wand confiscated. Licence to saw a woman in half revoked – blackballed by the Magicians' Union, basically.

I remember going to an event on London's South Bank in the mid '90s. It was when *Gummo* by Harmony Korine had just come out. There had been some controversy about the film so *Dazed & Confused* magazine arranged a screening & the filmmaker was there to defend it.

During the Q&A afterwards someone asked, 'How much of

the film was scripted, how much was improvised?' What was real
& what was staged? Perhaps a young film-maker hoping to get
some tips.

That's where I got this Magic Circle analogy from. Harmony
Korine point-blank refused to answer that question. He said it
would be like a magician revealing how he performed his tricks.
Not the done thing. It would be going against the Spirit of
Creation. Next question, please.

A lot of artists are superstitious about discussing their
creative process. They think that by discussing it they might
chase the muse away. They're scared of becoming creatively
impotent.

I read an interview with another film-maker, David Lynch,
in which he was asked if he'd ever been in therapy. He said that
he'd been to see a therapist once but, before the session began, he
asked whether being psychoanalysed might interfere with his
creativity. The therapist replied that, in all honesty, it might.
Lynch stood up to leave. 'Sorry, Doc – but that's a risk I'm not
prepared to take' were his parting words.

I witnessed a similar reaction, first-hand, when I spoke to
Leonard Cohen at the time of the release of his album *Old Ideas*
in 2012.

This meeting came about because, between 2011 & 2017, I
presented a radio show on BBC 6 Music called *Jarvis Cocker's
Sunday Service*. It was a dream job: for two hours every Sunday
afternoon I could play whatever music I liked – plus, I got to
speak to people who interested me. David Attenborough was
magisterial, John Hurt nearly walked out of the studio when I
began our conversation by discussing his drinking (schoolboy
error on my part), Marina Abramović made me re-evaluate the
performer–audience relationship – all these encounters were
fascinating glimpses into someone else's way of looking at the
world. I'm not a trained journalist – I would just turn the lights
in the studio way down low (people relax & open up more if
they don't have to worry about what they look like), put my

notebook on the desk in front of me (the only rule I made for myself was that I had to have at least ten questions written down on paper in advance of any interview) & start a conversation. More often than not I would get to the end of the interview & find that I hadn't referred to my pre-prepared notes at all. I still kept making them though. (I believe this is known in the trade as the 'Dumbo's Feather' school of journalism.)

I was nervous as hell about speaking to Leonard Cohen. I've been listening to his music for most of my life – he's the Master as far as I'm concerned – so the prospect of being in his company was pretty overwhelming.

That's another superstition that often gets trotted out: 'Never meet your heroes.' The reason presumably being that they'll turn out to be just another human being. That's exactly why I *do* want to meet people I admire: the fact that work you appreciate is made by a fellow human & not some alien super being is a source of inspiration to me. So when the call came in to host 'Mr Cohen's Album Launch' I accepted the invitation in a flash.

I did my homework. I listened to the record & noted lines in the lyrics that intrigued me. I dutifully wrote my ten questions in the back of my notebook. I put on my best jacket. I did everything I could to prepare myself. But, when the big day came around, I was still terrified.

Matters weren't helped by the fact that before the interview began I had to sit next to the man himself while the album was played back in its entirety to the audience. I hadn't been informed about this. It took me back to the fight I'd had at junior school. Here I was, gee-ed up & in the zone but now I had to sit in the dark for forty minutes before we could get down to it. This gave ample time for me to convince myself of the irredeemably banal nature of the questions I'd prepared. Plus, I was paranoid that he might interpret the slightest movement on my part as a criticism of the music we were listening to together. I've never sat so still in my life. Then, eventually, the lights went up. & the interview began . . .

I don't remember our exchange word for word. But Leonard Cohen proved to be as charming & friendly as I could ever have hoped for him to be. He was patient if I got lost in the middle of a question. He listened attentively & took time over his responses. He was a complete gentleman. But there was one subject he absolutely refused to be drawn on. The subject of his creativity.

This resistance became apparent when I attempted to discuss some of the lyrics on the new album. He fired a warning shot across my bows by saying, 'This is really a mysterious & somewhat dangerous territory we're moving into. I think if you look too deep into this process you probably end up in a kind of state of paralysis.'

That should have told me – but for some reason I pressed on, quoting a line from the song 'Banjo' which read:

There's something I've been watching, means a lot to me.
It's a broken banjo bobbing on a dark infested sea.

He looked me firmly in the eye & said, 'We've got to be very careful really exploring these sacred mechanics because somebody will throw a monkey wrench into the thing & we'll never write another line again, either of us.'

Ouch, I was holed below the waterline – I sounded the SOS & opened up the stage to questions from the floor.

The thing is, I really should have known better. Years ago, during an interview with a writer for a well-known rock magazine, I was asked what I thought of music journalism. I considered that for a while. Maybe I even looked him firmly in the eye. & then I told him he had the worst job in the world. Because he was spending his time asking musicians to explain how music works & none of us have got a clue. So he would never find the answers to the questions he was posing. He was on a pointless quest. He was wasting his life.

The resulting article didn't show me in a particularly favourable light (that's what you get for being honest) . . . But I really do believe that's the way it is. & that inability to explain how music & songwriting works is also what keeps musicians at it. It's magic.

So, I really don't want to get thrown out of the Magic Circle for over-explaining. I'm not writing this book to spoil the party. It's just that, for years now, in school halls after I've given a talk or backstage after a concert, people have come up and asked me how to go about becoming an artist. There's always a worried & needy expression on their faces when they ask that question. Like it's a really hard problem they're trying to solve. & my answer is: don't worry about *becoming* an artist – you already ARE ONE! You were wired up long ago. You've just got to keep the contacts clean & the juice flowing (which isn't as simple as it sounds, btw). Don't worry about where 'inspiration' is going to come from – it can come from anywhere & everywhere. The big question is: are you ready to receive it when it comes? Is your antenna up? Is your aerial extended? If so, you got mail . . . It's my motivational speech.

I'm writing this book because I want you to know that you're Magic, too. That's what gives me the temerity to consider these 'sacred mechanics' as Leonard Cohen so beautifully put it. I want you to recognise your own 'loam' – the soil that your ideas grow from. What you plant in there is up to you. & absolutely none of my business. But the rules are the same for everyone. It's not a mystery. It's a completely natural process. & a completely magical one. How about that for a combo?

& now, for my next trick . . .

Chapter Eleven

This may look like a snapshot
of six teenage boys piled on to
a settee but it's actually a band
photo. At least, it is in my mind.

We have moved downstairs, from the bedroom to the living room. I have decided to share the dream.

The people in the photo on the previous page are called Jarv, Fungus, Glen, Pip, Dolly & Dixie. Not all those are their given birth names. It's my equivalent of John, Paul, George & Ringo – the boys in the band.

I'd already been pretending that I was in a band for quite a while. It made school more interesting. 'The band entered the sports hall' was a more romantic idea to have pass through my mind than 'the group of six spotty teenagers entered the sports hall'. Being in a band was my way of joining a gang. I was no good at sports so that particular door to sociability was not open to me. We were just kids looking to have fun. & forming a band provided us with an opportunity to do that. At fifteen years old, I was the oldest involved.

Once we'd come up with the band name during the economics lesson the next step was to design a logo. Establish the b(r)and. Naturally I worked on this in the same exercise book we've been looking at. Here's one of my first attempts. 'Arabicus' takes up most of the space. 'Pulp' seems almost an afterthought at the bottom of the page. The fact that there's a line ruled all the way across the graph grid, rendering the image an (almost) square, suggests to me that this was intended to be an album cover design. (Talk about putting the cart before the horse – we hadn't even written any songs yet!) This hypothesis is supported by the extremely precise use of a ruler to write the word 'Arabicus': this was an image that was going to be scrutinised for years to come by 'fans' so it had to be done right – but is the 'u' floating in space below the 'c' & the 's' an intentional design feature? Or because the artist realised that he was running out of space as he approached the right-hand edge of the page? We may never know. I *do* know that the 'mystic eye' in the bottom left corner of the sleeve design was produced by tracing round a plectrum placed in varying positions. Tricks of the trade.

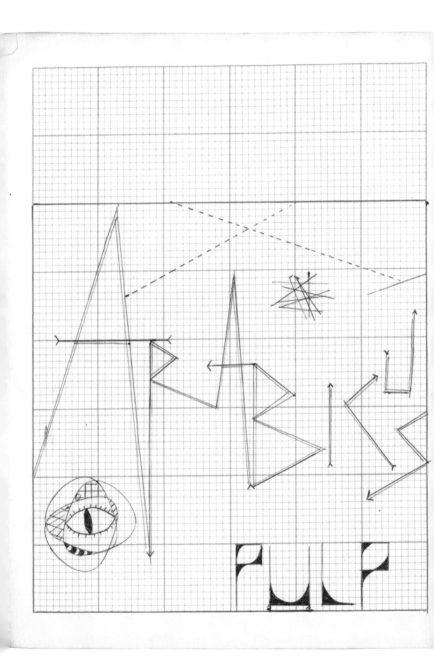

141

We have unearthed a very significant ring pull.

One of the members of the band, 'Dolly' (real name Peter Dalton), had a Saturday job in a supermarket. This meant that he could buy cans of lager even though he was only fourteen at the time. We arranged to buy a pallet of twenty-four cans between us & then use this as a lure to entice the other members of the band to attend a rehearsal at my mum's house one Friday night.

This dates from the era when the ring pull came off in your hand when you opened a can. You could then have lots of fun detaching the 'tongue' section & fitting it in one of the slits on the ring pull, which meant you could flick it at a friend/passer-by with quite an impressive amount of force. The fact that this ring pull has survived intact & 'unflicked' over the course of so many years makes it incredibly rare. KEEP.

Alcoholic enticement was necessary because some members of the band considered trying to play music the least pleasurable aspect of being in the group. You have to remember that no one had joined due to musical ability – more social availability: we were the kids with nothing else to do.

Only three people had turned up to our very first rehearsal. Me, Dolly & his younger brother Ian (who wasn't even in the band but it was the school holidays & Dolly wasn't allowed out of the house without him). We went round to my grandma & grandad's because there was an electric organ in their sitting room. Dolly 'played' the organ, I strummed the guitar & Ian banged on the coal scuttle because we didn't have any drums. A cassette tape of this very first rehearsal survives to this day. It's pretty unlistenable – there are no songs as such – it sounds more like we're having a competition to find out who can make the most noise. Perhaps unsurprisingly, the coal scuttle emerges victorious.

In my adult life I've hosted music classes with kids even younger than we were at the time. Pre-teens. First, I give them some instruments to play. Then I put my fingers in my ears. I've learnt that you have to resign yourself to the first ten minutes being an awful cacophony. The kids are excited that they're allowed to make noise without being told off so of course they're going to hit things & make as much of a racket as is humanly possible.

After ten minutes, generally speaking, the din begins to subside. Their arms are getting tired for a start. They may even be giving themselves a headache. & that's the time you can gently float the idea that perhaps they would like to play 'together' – even start listening to one another – & thus take the first, tentative steps towards making something referred to as 'music'.

Music is just organised noise.

We were crestfallen when we listened back to the cassette of that first rehearsal in my grandparents' front room. There was nothing 'organised' about the noise we heard. No songs had magically assembled themselves on the tape. Listening to it was a simultaneously painful yet extremely boring experience. All apart from one tiny moment, when a blinding shaft of sunlight had shone into the room, causing us all to stop playing for a few seconds & shield our eyes. I had cried out, 'Aaah, the Sun!' during this brief moment of silence. That was the only interesting section of the whole recording. It wasn't a song – but it was . . . something. It was a clue – a clue that being in a band was about cooperating, about making things happen at the same time, about pooling your efforts. It wasn't a competitive sport.

Armed with this knowledge we set up another rehearsal. This time at our house. My mum generally went out on Friday evenings so we arranged to rehearse from 8 p.m. till 10 p.m. Dolly brought the case of lager to ensure full attendance. My sister promised not to interfere. I locked the dog out in the garden so that he wouldn't get tangled up in the instrument cables. (All early Pulp rehearsal recordings feature the sound of a Staffordshire bull terrier whimpering to be let back in the house during quieter passages.)

One of the first songs we tried to learn was 'Stepping Stone' by The Monkees. I had done some advanced preparation & reckoned it had seven chords, which sounds like quite a lot if you apply the 'This is a chord, this is another, now go form a band' rule. But I had discovered a shortcut: the barre chord. A barre chord involves fingering a chord (in my case the 'E' chord) & then moving it up & down the neck of the guitar to play other chords, using your index finger to form a 'barre' at the appropriate fret. So to go from 'E' to 'A' you simply slide the same chord shape up to the fifth fret on the guitar. You can access all chords this way as long as you can jump to the appropriate fret quick enough. This was great news. I had improved on punk: 'This is ONE chord – now form a band.'

Nobody in the group knew the names of the notes on the instruments so I just called out the number of the appropriate fret to aim for. So 'Stepping Stone' was '5, 5, 8, 8, 10, 10, 13, 13' repeated three times, followed by once through '5, 5, 3, 3, 2, 2, 1, 1'. The neighbours might have thought there was a very rudimentary game of Bingo going on rather than a musical rehearsal.*

Songs with more complicated structures than this were beyond our grasp. So there was nothing for it but to try & write our own. &, because I had taken on the mantle of singer – & we were rehearsing in my house – & yes, in the end I suppose the band was my idea, it was up to me to get that particular ball rolling.

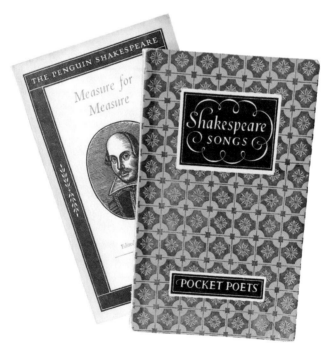

* Although my guitar playing has evolved over the years it's still largely based around this technique.

The first song I ever wrote was called 'Shakespeare Rock'. The opening verse goes like this:

> *I got a baby only one thing wrong*
> *She quote Shakespeare all day long*
> *I said, 'Baby, why you ignoring me?'*
> *She said, 'To be or not to be.'*

Followed by a chorus of:

> *Shakespeare Rock,*
> *Shakespeare Roll* [x2]

You have to remember that I was still at school. Being lumbered with writing song lyrics felt like being given extra homework. We were studying *Hamlet* in English class at the time. Maybe that's where the germ of the idea for the song came from. But, of course, there's more to it than that . . .

Writing your first song is a monumental undertaking. You're making a fundamental shift from being consumer to creator, from audience to performer. & the first big question you have to ask yourself is, 'What am I going to write about?' That's a very daunting question. Especially at the age of fifteen.

So I tried to turn the whole thing into a joke. That felt safer. Safer than writing about something personal & running the risk of being ridiculed by my friends. All my musical career up to this point had been conducted in private. Living in fear of being found out. I wasn't ready to 'come out' yet. So a joke song about something we were all finding boring at school seemed a good place to begin. I really wanted these rehearsals to continue – I needed the other members of the band not to lose interest.

It worked. 'Shakespeare Rock' was a hit – at least with the rest of the group – & we learnt how to play it together (in a manner of speaking) that night. We were a proper band!

Thus the template was established. We had two hours in

which to mess around & make a noise & drink cheap lager.*
Around a quarter to ten an elderly neighbour would ring up &
tell us that the noise we were making was aggravating her
shingles. The dog would whine & rub his nose against the glass
of the French windows until we eventually let him back into the
house. This was our Friday-night routine for the next one & a
half years.

---

* Actually, the lager got phased out after a while as it turned out to be a little
counter-productive.

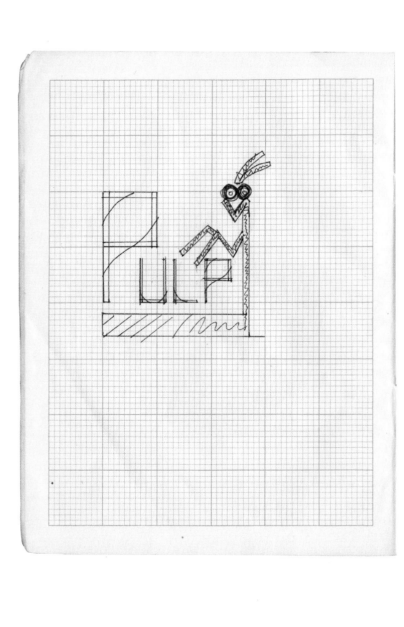

Chapter Twelve

Pulp once had a mascot: a praying mantis.

The logo on the previous page was a victory for me. 'Arabicus' has gone and only 'Pulp' remains – which is what I'd always wanted the band name to be. But to get my way I'd had to learn one of the rules of being in a band: the rule of compromise. In this case the Mantis Compromise.

The first bass player in the group was David 'Fungus' Lockwood. He's the Queen fan that I mentioned earlier in the book who tried to grow a moustache so he could look like Freddie Mercury. He actually did a pretty good job of realising this ambition because, physically, he was an early developer. By age fourteen he could pass for being in his mid-twenties. This was ironic because he was also the most wilfully immature (or 'imma' as we put it in those days) member of the band. Quite a combination.

For example: he didn't last long as the band's bass player due to his 'speeding'. I'm not talking about drug abuse here: he viewed playing each song as a race. After I'd done the time-honoured '1, 2, 3, 4' count-in, he would play all the notes in his bass line as quickly as possible, then shout, 'Finished!' & put his instrument down. The rest of the band would be somewhere back around the first chorus mark. Left in the dust. Of course, this was hilarious the first time he did it. A stroke of comic genius – but then he KEPT DOING IT. It was thus decided that Fungus should take on a more 'conceptual' position within the group. & his major contribution in this role was to come up with the idea of a praying mantis as group mascot/visual signifier. He had been against losing 'Arabicus' from the band name & would only accept it on three conditions:

1. 'Arabicus' is replaced by the graphic representation of a mantis.
2. Pulp's (so far imaginary) records are released through 'Mantis Inc.'
3. The mantis's name is Obidiah.

Sounds perfectly reasonable – where do I sign?

Thus the band developed through a slow process of compromise & collaboration. Members came & went. Fungus & Glen concentrated on the visual side of the band. They produced sweatshirts with the new mantis-enhanced logo on them. Glen borrowed his dad's Super 8 cine camera & made two 'Mantis Inc.' productions featuring members of the band & other school friends. The first, *The Three Spartans*, was a remake of an obscure historical B-movie called *The 300 Spartans*. The second was called *Star Trek (with Spaghetti Western Overtones)* & involved the crew of the *Starship Enterprise* beaming down to a planet where everyone was a character from a Spaghetti Western. I got the Clint Eastwood role – mainly due to the fact that I'd been given some cowboy boots as a present by an aunt the previous Christmas. Plus, my mum let me borrow her knitted poncho.

We also found time to write more songs. They were still pretty jokey. Dolly came up with a tongue-in-cheek pro-royalist response to the Sex Pistols' 'Anarchy in the UK' called 'Monarchy in the UK'. We had another called 'Message from the Martians' that stole the bass line from Joy Division's 'New Dawn Fades' & featured Fungus making 'alien noises' whilst my sister improvised on the viola she'd just started learning at school. Rehearsals were still cacophonous in the main part but, as with that tiny 'the Sun!' interlude that happened during our very first rehearsal in my grandparents' front room, there were occasional moments of clarity when things would gel & sound . . . musical. & the really good news was that these moments kept getting longer.

We were making progress.

The *John Peel Show* continued to be a primary influence. Apart from appropriating a Joy Division bass line I was very inspired by The Cure's first album, *Three Imaginary Boys*. The sparse & basic instrumentation & production gave me hope that we could achieve similar results with our limited resources. I tried to mimic Robert Smith's extremely 'tinny' guitar sound &

we turned down the tone knob on the bass guitar to make it more 'bassy'. Because the bass was going through a cheap plastic 5-watt amplifier this actually led to it sounding more 'farty' because it overloaded the speaker, but we decided we liked the effect. 'Tinny guitar, farty bass, clattery drums' became our signature sound – our homage to the first Cure album.

Of course, John Peel's very favourite record was 'Teenage Kicks' by The Undertones. & when that came out in 1978 we had been just as captivated by it as the rest of Peel's audience. So much so that Dolly stole the opening guitar riff & used it in a song of his that he brought to one of our Friday-night sessions. The song was called 'Queen Poser' & though the words were still not up to much (sample lyric: 'Poses for the men in all the trendy clubs / Never relaxes by going down the pub') we all agreed that it was our best yet. It sounded like a 'real' song (perhaps the fact that 50 per cent of it came from a song that had already been a hit had something to do with that). All this thrashing around in the dark actually seemed to be leading somewhere.

This is the ideal way to start a musical career – exploring unknown territories with a bunch of friends. That's why I've tried to preserve that spirit of adventure in any of the musical education classes I've hosted in later life. The great thing about working with a group of kids is seeing that enthusiasm which makes them simply want to make noise on an instrument. Feeling their excitement when they get that instrument to 'work' in any which way they can. I always try to operate in this spirit because that's how new things can happen. Maybe they'll come up with a way of using an instrument that would never occur to an adult musician. With no ulterior motive – just through the sheer joy of making a noise.

&, as I discovered all those years ago, if you keep on playing, eventually that chaos will begin to coalesce into something concrete. You can't help it. You'll simply get bored of making noise all the time & naturally make the effort needed to turn it into something that could be called a 'song'. It's inevitable. It's the logical next step. It might take a couple of months, it might take a year, but if you do keep at it eventually you will end up with not only one song – but maybe as many as nine or ten.

In other words: A Set.

& this is the time when you begin to think, 'Could we do this in front of other people?' Make it real. Make it 'official'.

It was after about a year & a half of aggravating the neighbour's shingles every Friday night that Pulp played their first-ever concert. At City Comprehensive School during a Wednesday lunch break in March 1980.

That's how long it took for our noise to solidify, enabling us to take that next, giant leap.

Chapter Thirteen

Stardom awaits.

It's a while since we've considered a clothing item so let's take a look at this. This is a Star Jumper – these were a fashion craze in the period immediately before punk happened. The label inside reads 'TOPSPIN – made in Hong Kong from 100 per cent acrylic fibre'. These jumpers were everywhere at our school – usually paired with Birmingham Bags, which were trousers with giant wide legs.

You may have heard of 'Oxford Bags' – tweed trousers originally worn by Oxford undergraduates in the 1920s. Well, Birmingham Bags were a lower-class version, made out of polyester & worn by kids in comprehensive schools in the mid-'70s. The other difference was they had pockets halfway down the legs. Like army trousers. Nobody ever used these pockets. You would have had to walk around the school like a hunchback just to get your hands in them. Not the desired effect. They also had a three-button high waist. Two sets of three buttons sewn about six inches apart on the waistband. This Star Jumper is really tight & also has a high, ribbed waist. So imagine the combination of this very skinny top half with the voluminous wide legs & platform shoes below. It was definitely a strong look.

I've heard it said that these wide trousers caught on because they gave Northern Soul dancers the freedom of movement needed to execute their extreme dance moves. Moves like that swallow dive that I fell foul of at the teenage party I mentioned earlier.

It was funny to watch kids wearing Birmingham Bags walking to school when it was windy because the legs of the trousers would flap about violently. It was even more amusing when people rode motorbikes whilst wearing them. You could hear this flapping effect coming up behind you from miles away. Like some giant mechanical bird desperately attempting to take off.

I wore neither a Star Jumper nor a pair of Birmingham Bags to school whilst they were 'in' because my mother thought they were both 'over-priced garbage'. She may have had a point – but I was disappointed because I was still in my pre-punk 'I want to fit in' phase.

I eventually bought myself a Star Jumper from a jumble sale, by which time they were well out of style. I wore it on a couple of occasions as an anti-fashion/anti-parental authority statement.

The fact that I could even conceive of such a thing as an 'anti-fashion statement' at the time is all down to the man pictured opposite.

Mark E. Smith isn't wearing an actual Star Jumper in this early photo of The Fall. But it's definitely from the same family. The Fall were John Peel's favourite band. He loved the way they always did their own thing & were impervious to prevailing trends in the music scene. Mark E. Smith's look perfectly encapsulates this attitude: the band started releasing music in the immediate aftermath of punk but their image is definitely not that of a standard punk group. By wearing a 100 per cent acrylic jumper that, a matter of months before, had been the epitome of mainstream fashion, Mark E. Smith is 'calling out' the punk orthodoxy that had already begun to manifest itself. After all, punk was supposed to be about inventing yourself & not being a sheep. & a 100 per cent acrylic pullover certainly has nothing to do with a sheep.

I'd experienced the conservative side of punk first-hand myself when I went to a Stranglers concert in 1979. I wasn't there just to get beard inspiration from their lead singer / guitarist Hugh Cornwell, The Stranglers were the first punk band I'd really got into. (You'll remember, their *Rattus Norvegicus* was the second album I ever bought.)

I couldn't persuade any of my school friends to come to the concert with me so I ended up going alone. I was wearing a flecked tweed jacket from a jumble sale, a plain shirt, some

159

sand-coloured drainpipe jeans handed down from an older cousin & a blue crocheted tie my mother had knitted for me when I first went to primary school. This caused some consternation among the leather-jacketed, spiky-haired guys in front of me in the queue to get into the venue. They accused me of being a 'mod'. I was surprised & disappointed – & scared because they looked pretty hard. As far as I was concerned punk meant anything goes. It was against the herd mentality & for freedom of personal expression. & if that meant wearing a badly crocheted blue tie, so be it. At least I wasn't wearing a uniform like them. Of course, I didn't express any of this out loud – I just moved to the back of the queue & kept my head down.

This was the first big concert I'd been to. I was amazed to see that the area immediately in front of the stage was completely empty. I walked up to the crowd barrier & stood right in the centre. Best view in the house. This was going to be awesome. I was joined by a few more audience members when the support band came on but then the crowd soon thinned out again when they finished & people went back to the bar. My sense of anticipation was mounting. I was soon going to see my favourite band play live for the very first time! From the front row! The lights went down & an intro tape began to play.

& then something very scary happened.

As the band took to the stage & played their first notes a vast horde of black-clad people rushed to the front of the venue & began to jump up & down. I was crushed very hard against the crowd barrier so I tried to push back into the mass of bodies. I managed to move a few yards away from the barrier but then something even more unnerving happened: my feet were no longer touching the ground. I wasn't levitating – I was in a mosh pit. The only thing stopping me falling to the ground & being crushed underfoot was the fact that the heaving crowd was so closely packed together there was no room to fall. It was like treading water in an extremely stormy sea that smelt of BO. I was terrified. I turned away from the stage & struggled for the shoreline – (otherwise known as the back wall of the venue). I spent the rest of the concert in this safe haven, watching an identikit mass of spiky-haired young men attempting to pogo in front of me. They were like a gang of the tough kids at school who liked football. This was a punk crowd?

I saw Mark E. Smith 'critique' this caricature version of punk at another concert I went to a few months after that Stranglers show. John Peel had played loads of tracks from The Fall's *Live at the Witch Trials* so when I saw they were going to play The Polytechnic in Sheffield I decided I had to go. This time I managed to persuade my sister to come with me. Me & Saskia generally had a similar musical taste – but that all changed when we saw The Fall. She absolutely hated them – she said she 'didn't even think it was music'. Although I passionately disagreed with her I could kind of get where she was coming from. The Fall took punk's challenge to invent something new seriously. In their case that meant questioning the very notion of what music could be. Did it have to be in time? Did the instruments have to be in tune? Did the 'singer' actually have to sing? & were you really allowed to put '-ah' at the end of every word? The only lyrics I could decipher during the entire concert were 'male slags [or, more accurately, 'male slags-ah'] in tight black pants'. I still say that sometimes when I visit my sister to wind her up.

Unlike her, I loved the whole evening. It was another beacon of hope. As a member of a band that often had issues with timing, tuning & all that jazz it was inspiring to see that it didn't necessarily need to be a setback. It was 'character'. The Fall took those rough edges that normally get edited out of a performance & placed them centre-stage. Forced you to listen to them & acknowledge their importance. Made you re-evaluate what a song could be. My eyes (& ears) were opened. My head expanded. I'm still grateful.

Mark E. Smith's run-in with the punk purists came towards the end of the concert. He was looking into the crowd & he spotted a female fan dressed up to the nines in the 'correct' punk clothing. 'Ooh, look – it's Siouxsie Sioux! Hello, Siouxsie,' he deadpanned. He himself was wearing the kind of leather box-jacket you would see on a bloke down the bookies. It was a pivotal moment for me. The realisation that dressing straight or square was more subversive than actively trying to shock. That aspect of punk had got old really fast – it was just too easy to copy & caricature. Dyed hair, safety pins – yawn. Mark E. Smith 'shocked' by going under the radar, in deep cover like a plain-clothes cop. Leaving it up to the music to shock people. That concert at The Polytechnic was everything that The Stranglers show hadn't been. I was a convert. I bought the Star Jumper very soon afterwards. & when one of the first live reviews of Pulp said that we sounded like 'a cross between Abba & The Fall' I was beyond proud.

But now I'm getting ahead of myself . . .

Before I get on with telling you the story o
Pulp's very first concert I'd like to take a
commercial break.

Let's watch some telly.

Look what I've found: This is a JVC 3020 U)
television. I don't know if you can get a prope
sense of scale from the picture but the thing
about this television is that it's really tiny
The screen is about four inches wide and two
& a half inches tall.

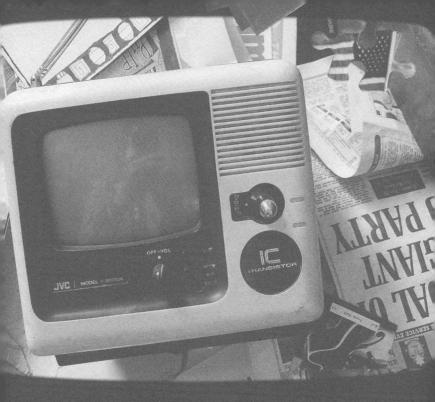

Small Telly –
Big Influence.

Mass ownership of a television set was still quite a recent development at the time, but as I was brought up with one, I couldn't imagine life being any different. We've already established how pliable & receptive young children's minds are. It all goes in. & then a lot of it stays there.

(Radio) November 19, 1964. Vol. 155. No. 2141.

I've long been fascinated by trying to quantify just how much of a formative influence this early exposure to TV has been on me. Mainly due to some poor Life Decisions I feel could be attributed to it. Here's a still from a stage show called *Room 29* that I devised in collaboration with the pianist Chilly Gonzales back in 2016 to investigate this very subject. That's him on the left of the picture seated at the piano – I'm towards the right of the image, trapped inside the TV set (symbolic).

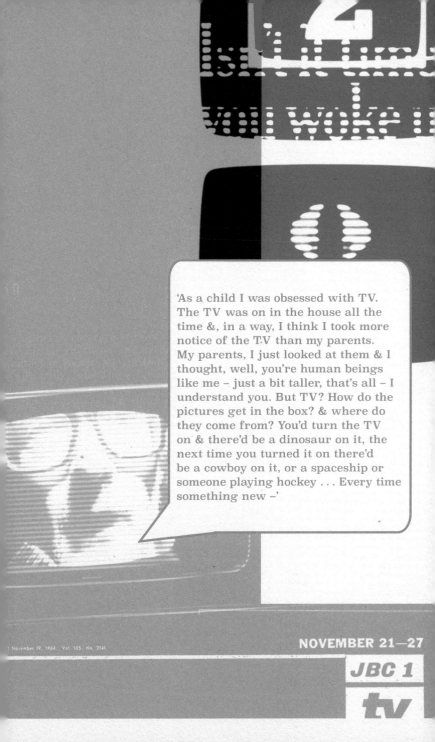

As a young (pre-glasses) child, by sitting at the right distance away from the screen, I had been able to see this mysterious televisual world in perfect detail. Then, as soon as I took my eyes off the screen, the world went out of focus. So maybe it's not that hard to understand why I took more notice of the TV than my parents.

I think my mother must have eventually cottoned on to this subversive influence in our household because she devised a cunning way of 'taking back control'. She rented a coin-operated television set.

Though I've mentioned this to friends over the years I'm still yet to meet anyone else who grew up with one of these contraptions in their living room so you're just going to have to take my word for it. It was a black-&-white TV in a white plastic housing – completely indistinguishable from any other TV of the period, except for the fact that it had a large black metal box with a coin slot bolted to the back of it. You put a ten-pence piece in the slot, turned a dial until you heard it drop into the box & then the television would spark to life. You could then gawp to your heart's content until the credit ran out about an hour later.

Welcome to the world of addiction: I would watch EVERYTHING, no matter what it was, because I had paid for it. Then, when the screen suddenly went dark (accompanied by a gentle 'ping'), I would instantly be plagued by pangs of withdrawal. Followed by a mad dash around the house to find a coin for my next fix.

PROGRAMMES IN COLOUR THIS WEEK

from the JBC transmitter

30 20

The intended purpose of this Cash Box Goggle Box was of course not to turn kids into rabid Telly Addicts but to help with the price of paying the TV licence fee (a man would come round once a month to empty the box for that purpose), but this association between TV viewing & money gave television an illicit appeal. Turned it into something like one of those peep-show machines they used to have at the fairground where you put a coin in & cranked the handle to see a woman taking her clothes off. The credit always ran out just before there was any nudity. & our home TV was now just like that: when the screen abruptly went blank you couldn't help but feel you were missing out on something big. The good bit you'd been patiently waiting for. That kept me hooked.

So my mother's attempt at parental discipline really only ended up reinforcing my addiction.

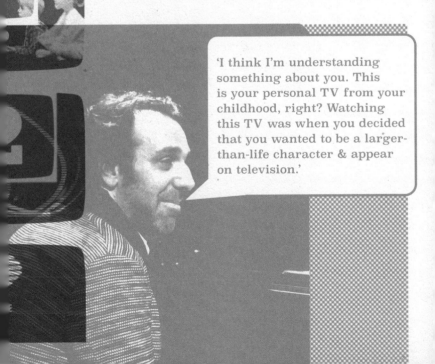

'I think I'm understanding something about you. This is your personal TV from your childhood, right? Watching this TV was when you decided that you wanted to be a larger-than-life character & appear on television.'

Well, the TV screen was certainly the first place I saw people performing music. Years & years before I saw a live concert I was an avid viewer of the BBC show *Top of the Pops*. That is the way I first saw music performed: for the camera. With all the business that entails. Gonzales also tells the story of how when he first saw me performing on stage he was reminded of seeing a twelve-year-old kid trying to emulate the moves of his favourite pop stars as learnt from TV.

So I don't find it surprising that when Pulp actually got to perform on *Top of the Pops* many years later (Life Goals, etc.), I insisted on miming my singing rather than doing it live. Because to me that felt more authentic. That was how all the performers had done it when I was a kid. Miming was 'keeping it real' as far as I was concerned. The rest of the band would be miming anyway so why not me?

(Of course, back in the day, some punk bands had protested against this 'phoney' nature of *TOTP*. That's why The Clash never performed on the show. & I remember The Stranglers being on once & JJ Burnel 'playing' a bass with no strings on it. That was his 'real'. But to me he was missing the point: Pop had nothing to do with reality – it was an improvement on reality.)

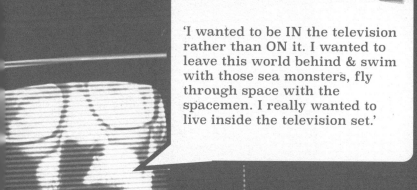

'I wanted to be IN the television rather than ON it. I wanted to leave this world behind & swim with those sea monsters, fly through space with the spacemen. I really wanted to live inside the television set.'

& when I was a kid I thought the way you got to be inside the box was by becoming famous. So, if I could become a pop star I would be granted access to TV Land. & I would finally be able to swim with the dolphins & ride the Wild Frontier.

In *Room 29* I got to realise this childhood fantasy (quite literally, as you can see from the photo) – & in the safe, controlled environment of a theatre. It hasn't been quite so neat & tidy in real life though. Preferring images on a TV screen to real life is obviously going to cause some 'issues'. Especially with the people near to you in that real life. I've consciously been trying to wean myself off TV for quite a number of years now.

I feel I've come a long way – but every day is a struggle. If I'm staying in a hotel I'll put a blanket over the screen so that I'm not tempted to turn the TV set on. When my son was younger I would tape drawings of his over the screen to the same end. Lead us not into temptation. & if I walk into a room or a bar and there's a television on in the corner, I still can't stop myself from looking at it. That's awkward if I'm out to meet friends because I will end up staring into the corner rather than paying attention to them. Rude, even. But I really can't help it. It dates back to those days when television was a magical, semi-forbidden device that beamed visions of another world into my everyday reality. It's hard to ignore something that once did that. Maybe I'm still hoping to catch the good bit.

I guess the best thing you could say about the JVC 3020 television is that it's 'portable'. That was handy when I was moving between households a lot. That convenience came with a payback though: for instance, trying to watch televised snooker on it was a real waste of time. First of all, it's a black-&-white TV so you couldn't see what colour the balls were, making it hard to follow the game.

That was irritating enough but the really insurmountable problem was that the bottom two pockets on the snooker table disappeared below the edge of the moulded black plastic surround. So you could never really tell whether or not someone had potted anything when the ball went down that end of the table. Obviously not a TV designed by a fan of the sport some call 'chess with balls'.

That should have alerted me really: television doesn't show you the full picture. But I was still years away from learning that particular life lesson.

OK, end of 'A Message from our Sponsors', but an understanding of the extent of my TV addiction is an essential part of this story. It's where a lot of my initial ideas about the world came from. A major constituent of my 'loam'. The place I got all my information about what a pop performance should be, for a start.

Which hopefully helps set the scene well enough for you to understand why the very first Pulp concert was such an unmitigated disaster.

Chapter
Fourteen

I designed this ticket for the first-ever Pulp concert. The logo is there, Obidiah the mantis is there. Twenty pence for 'APPROX. 30 MINS OF LIVE! PULP'.

Playing our first concert during lunch break at school was both logical & practical. We had no idea of how to get on the live band circuit in Sheffield. Plus, we were too young to go in places that served alcohol. &, no one would have come to see us because nobody knew who we were. People at school knew who we were – we were 'The Weirdos'.

We had a bit of a reputation within the school because we'd already presented the two films masterminded by Fungus & Glen during another lunch break a few months earlier. Glen spliced *The Three Spartans* & *Star Trek (with Spaghetti Western Overtones)* together with a few spoof adverts & a promo for 'Shakespeare Rock' (that featured Fungus, Dixie & myself playing volleyball with one of my sister's dolls) on to one film reel. The films were silent so during one of our Friday-night rehearsals Glen set up his dad's Super 8 film projector & screen in our living room & we all gathered around the In Tensai Rhythm Machine & dubbed a live voiceover track. It took a couple of attempts for us to get through the whole thing without cracking up laughing but eventually we managed a 'pass' that we were happy with & spent the rest of the evening watching it back. It was pretty good – even though it was always a bit out of sync because it was difficult to start the cassette player & the film projector at exactly the same time.

Word got round the school that we had 'made a film'. The coolest teacher in City Comprehensive School was our maths teacher Mr Jarvis (good name). Mr Jarvis had long hair & a wispy beard & was into 'progressive' music like Van der Graaf Generator. He got wind of our film & suggested that we might want to screen it for the other pupils. He could clear it with the powers that be. Yes, please.

& so, a few weeks later, we found ourselves in the wings of the stage in the school assembly hall at around 12.30 in the afternoon in a state of heightened nervous excitement. Part of that excitement was just standard, teenage energy but another part of it was pure fear. In the intervening weeks since Mr Jarvis had made his suggestion we had tried really hard to solve the problem of syncing the film's soundtrack to the image. We drew marks on the film leader of the Super 8 reel, we rewound the soundtrack cassette to a certain point & pressed 'zero' on the tape counter. Then we would count down from five, pressing the 'start' button on both machines simultaneously when we reached 'zero'. But it was still hit & miss. & these experiments had always been conducted with us all in close proximity. Now I was up in the wings of the stage with the cassette player & Glen was miles away at the back of the hall with the cine projector! We couldn't even see each other, let alone hear each other. How was this going to work?

The hall was filling up. Such an event was a novelty. Everyone was curious to see what the weirdos had been up to. The scraping of metal-framed chairs on the parquet flooring of the assembly hall slowly began to die down as people took their seats. 12.30 was approaching fast. I was petrified. We were going to show ourselves up in front of the whole school. We'd never live it down. Help. In desperation Dolly volunteered to stand at the edge of the stage curtain & do a two-armed semaphore countdown: one arm visible to me backstage, the other to Glen at the back of the hall. It was our only chance. Zero hour was upon us. No escape. Dolly took up his position. The room went quiet. My finger hovered over the 'pause' button of the cassette player.

5,4,3,2,1...

The film was a resounding success. By some miracle the soundtrack was perfectly in sync with the image. Better than we'd ever got it during any of our dry runs. People laughed. They even clapped at the end. It was a triumph. We were in business!

By now the band line-up had solidified into: me on guitar & vocals, Jimmy Sellars on drums, Jamie Pinchbeck on bass & vocals, & Peter 'Dolly' Dalton on guitar, keyboards & vocals. The photograph opposite does NOT show us in our stage gear. (There was a roving photographer at the school Christmas fancy dress party & we took the opportunity to get a free band photo.) Head waiter, gangster, Bunny Girl & Rupert the Bear – that would be quite a line-up.

Jimmy had joined because Mark 'Dixie' Swift left to be in the school football team. We poached Jamie from a Black Sabbath-influenced heavy metal band at school called Satan. His mum worked at a hairdresser's in the row of shops in front of our house.

Encouraged by the success of the film show we asked if we could play a concert at school, also at lunchtime, & got the thumbs-up.

'30 MINS OF LIVE! PULP' might not sound that much but it's a tall order when your audience up to date has consisted of a dog & an infirm neighbour. The leap to live performance is intimidating. It's the difference between talking to yourself & addressing a crowd. A quantum leap. We thought we sounded good in the living room but apart from the aforementioned dog, neighbour & (occasionally) my sister there were no witnesses to back up our story. What would it be like to perform in front of other people? We knew it was the next step in the band's evolution, but that didn't stop it being a very scary prospect. At least the fact that the film had gone down well gave us a little confidence.

In fact, the success of the film show had opened some doors. Mr Jarvis volunteered to record the concert on his 4-Track reel-to-reel tape recorder. So now it was going to be not only our first concert but also our first album! We began to dream big: I decided we needed pyrotechnics. We approached the head of the chemistry department & he agreed to help us out. Then I spotted some brightly coloured material in one of the school stock cupboards & asked if we could have it to make stage costumes. The answer was once again yes. Everybody seemed to be on our side.

Alarm bells should have been ringing. Over the years I've learnt to recognise this as dangerous behaviour: this tendency to 'over-egg the pudding' as some might put it. It's good to want to put on a show – give people something to look at – but it's dangerous when it becomes a way of distracting yourself from the real task in hand. The bottom line was that I was shit-scared of going on stage & was hoping that no one would notice if there was enough smoke wafting about & we wore bright costumes.

& the costumes definitely were bright. I was really into the band Devo at the time & they all wore matching paper boiler suits which I thought looked cool. The material I'd found in the school stock cupboard consisted of one roll featuring a floral pattern on a red background & another of a shiny green textured synthetic material. My guess is that they were either upholstery or curtain fabric. Most definitely not 'cool'. I took the rolls of material home & persuaded my sister to make up some outfits

using my mum's sewing machine. Her seamstress skills were rudimentary so she made short-sleeved tops with slash necks & pyjama-style trousers with elasticated waists. We only wore the full costumes for that very first concert. No pictures exist of that performance – but I'm wearing a pair of the trousers in the photo opposite taken a few months later.

Imagine those trousers paired with a shiny, lime-green crop top. It was certainly a 'look'.

Now my memory begins to get hazy. Over the years I've told many interviewers that I have very little recollection of live concerts. Especially if they're good. They seem to almost take place without my involvement. The music uses you as a conduit for a couple of hours & then goes on its way. But this first concert was not good. How could it be? With all it had riding on it. The over-ambitious stage show. The ill-advised costumes. The live recording. Not exactly a 'soft launch'. Talk about setting yourself up for a fall. & I think the trauma of that fall is what led to it being almost completely erased from my memory.

I say 'almost completely erased' because there are one or two details I can remember. One is the 'pyrotechnics'.

This idea had come from some experiments with magnesium ribbon in chemistry class. As any secondary-school pupil knows, if you ignite magnesium ribbon it burns with an intense white light, produces quite a lot of smoke & leaves behind a powdery residue called magnesium oxide (which is used in indigestion remedies). We weren't interested in manufacturing our own brand of artisanal Milk of Magnesia – it was the intense white light & smoke we were after. Bands on *Top of the Pops* had smoke & lighting effects so we needed some too. In the enclosed environment of the chemistry classroom we'd all had to wear protective goggles when conducting the experiment & the teacher had told us not to look directly at the burning flame (so of course we all did). It was like looking at the brightest sparkler ever. What a perfect start to a concert.

The problem was, the school assembly hall was about thirty times bigger than the chemistry classroom – & our chemistry teacher & his two assistant pupils had set up their makeshift 'lab' towards the rear of the stage area. When they took to the stage wearing white lab coats, ignited their solitary Bunsen burner & lit the magnesium ribbon the effect was distinctly underwhelming. Especially because we'd forgotten to close the curtains in the hall. It was more 'impromptu daytime chemistry class' than 'Good evening, Wembley!' & then the band 'burst' on to the stage wearing a set of pensioners' curtains. In broad daylight. In front of the whole school. Complete & utter humiliation. The memory still makes me shudder.

& it was all downhill from there. We never recovered from that embarrassing damp squib of a start.

Going on stage can be like entering another dimension – you construct the dream inside your head & then you live out that fantasy in front of the audience. When it all works there is no feeling like it – but it only takes one little technical hitch or mistake to bring you crashing back down to earth &, once you're there, it can be very difficult to get in the zone again. & there are so many things that can go wrong on stage. All it takes is a loose instrument lead or a guitar going out of tune for the spell you've cast to be broken.

Over the years I've got better at dealing with these inevitable glitches – but I've certainly learnt the hard way:

A few years after the school hall debacle we are playing a show at the Library Theatre in Sheffield. It's our biggest concert to date. Everything is going well until I get animated in one song & my glasses fall off. As we have established, I am pretty much blind without my glasses. I drop to my knees & start feeling my way around the stage, hoping to retrieve them. No luck. Other members of the band put down their instruments & join in the search. Still no luck. It's like a very intense anxiety dream. The audience are starting to get restless. Where the hell are my glasses? After what feels like a lifetime the drummer finds them – inside his bass drum! Which is nothing short of a miracle because the front skin on his bass drum has just one small round hole cut into it to allow the insertion of a microphone, leaving a space of maybe two inches through which my glasses have somehow managed to find their way. It's a trick David Blaine or Dynamo would be proud of. But the ten minutes or so it has taken

to discover the glasses' whereabouts have unfortunately dissolved any 'magic' we may have conjured up in the auditorium &, try as we might, we never get it back.

Solution

1) Keeping head immobile whilst on stage (impractical)
2) Contact lenses (worked well for a while but led to medical issues)
3) Elasticated spectacle strap – still in use today.

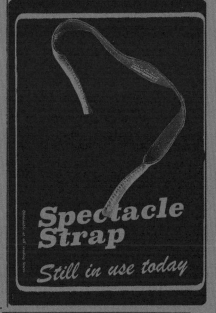

Spectacle Strap
Still in use today

02: TOMMY, CAN YOU HEAR ME?

As well as being an instrument a microphone is also a prop – something for a singer to play with on stage – & for this reason I always use a microphone with a cable rather than a modern wireless mic. The cable makes the microphone a lot more versatile – you can drape it over your shoulder, hang it round your neck, let the microphone hang loose during an instrumental passage. One famous example of 'stagecraft' only possible with a cabled microphone is the practice, popularised by Roger Daltrey of The Who, of swinging the microphone around your head like a cowboy with a lasso. It's a classic 'rock' trope. I've never tried this one myself but I have witnessed the lead singer of a well-known band (who shall remain nameless) come a cropper whilst trying to 'do a Daltrey'.

I was at the NME Awards a few years ago. (It must have been a few years ago because the event was being televised on network TV.) The television production company had hired quite an intimate venue because they were going for an 'authentic, sweaty, rock & roll' kind of feel. Edgy – yet well-lit. The stage was only about a foot off the ground. We guests were seated at round tables, the nearest of which were just a yard or so from the front edge of the stage. Like I said, intimate.

The band in question take to the stage exuding as much attitude as they can muster. Especially the singer. As his bandmates start playing an intro he begins twirling the microphone around his head. The people on the front tables have to duck down. The scene somehow reminds me of being at a bird-of-prey display at a village fete – that moment when the bird handler sets an eagle free & it flies off into the distance. Then the handler blows a whistle & whips a length of string with a piece of meat tied to the end of it through the air to lure the bird back. All spectators immediately cower with their arms above their heads for protection, fearing the bird's return. The scene in front of the stage is similar (minus the bird of prey obviously). I'm glad I'm sitting a few rows back. I can't get too complacent though: the singer is gradually letting out more of the mic cable & the 'circumference of danger' is increasing. The band members behind him are now having to move back towards their amplifiers to stay out of the way. It's becoming obvious that this scenario has not been rehearsed in advance. They've been playing that intro riff for at least a minute now. I'm trying to read the expression on the singer's face. He's troubled – he doesn't know how to reel the mic back in so that he can start singing. As long as he keeps the momentum going the microphone will remain airborne – but how do you keep that momentum going whilst simultaneously reeling the mic in so you can begin the song?

There's no time to further ponder the physics of the situation – the answer comes in the form of the unmistakable clunk of the microphone hitting something hard (a table, not a human head, fortunately) & then dragging noisily along the floor. The room is silent. The

music has stopped. The singer is trying to brazen it out by staring at the back wall of the venue. The audience are breathing a sigh of relief. I am trying so hard to contain my laughter that I feel I may be in danger of wetting myself.

Here endeth the lesson.

Back during that school lunch break at the beginning of the 1980s I was years away from learning these valuable life (or should that be 'live'?) lessons. All I knew was that things weren't going at all the way I'd imagined them. & the more I thought about that, the more distracted I got, leading to yet more mistakes. Mistakes get edited out of TV – the reason you're not familiar with that 'epic Roger Daltrey fail' scenario I just described. I was learning the hard way that this wasn't TV. There was no second take. We were in a helpless spiral into a bottomless pit of teenage despair.

Mercifully, as I stated earlier, I have no recollection of the rest of the concert. The memory has been erased. Just like the live recording of the show that Mr Jarvis made on his 4-Track. When he brought it up during our next maths lesson I begged him to wipe the tape. 'Don't you want a souvenir of your very first live concert?' he asked incredulously. 'If I do get rid of it I'm sure you'll regret it in later life.' But I was adamant – I could not bear the thought of our moment of utter humiliation being preserved for posterity. The sound of a dream crashing to the ground. Who would ever want to listen back to that? I was convinced the group was over. We had failed our audition. Now I was never going to find out what it was like to live in TV Land. So, erase the tape. Destroy the evidence. Rewrite history. As far as I was concerned it was The Day That Never Happened.

The page from the exercise book shown opposite bears witness to this Stalinist purge: Pulp's Year Zero is listed as Saturday 5 July 1980 – the date we supported a band called 'The Naughtiest Girl Was a Monitor' at Rotherham Arts Centre. There's no mention of the concert we played at school only a couple of months before. Revisionism in action.

(By the way, Mr Jarvis reluctantly complied with my request &, yes, of course I DO now regret not having that tape. Subsequent experiences have taught me that it probably wasn't as bad as I thought it was. Nothing ever is.)

CONCERT LIST

1/ Rotherham Arts Centre with
Naughtiest Girl was a Monitor.
5/7/80

2/ Leadmill with 8 others
16/8/80

3/ Hallamshire with B-Troop and
un-named support group 17/8/80.

4/ Hallamshire with Detective Turtles
& Mark Mywords. 31/8/80 (Tape)
(Freak out on my part. Enjoyable)

5/ Royal with Vital (we were bad)
24/9/80 (Tape)

6/ LIMIT with B Troop & Y?"
Only knew we were playing 2 hrs before
we went on. 30/9/80. (Good)

7/ Hallamshire with Flying Alphonso
Brothers. Only knew at 4.00pm same
day.
9/10/80

Chapter Fifteen

The shirts keep coming.

This is a goodie – at one point the shirt pictured on the previous page was my favourite item of stage wear. &, this time, it did NOT come from a jumble sale. My grandparents brought it back as a gift for me from a Greek holiday. I was completely astounded. I was expecting a reproduction of a Grecian urn or a plaster model of the Acropolis, not the COOLEST SHIRT EVER. & in a breathable polycotton-mix fabric to boot.

How to describe the pattern on the shirt? 'Orange spiral constellations on a background of beige cloud nebulae floating in the infinity of deep green space' doesn't even begin to do it justice. It's the 'Stargate' sequence from *2001* in shirt form – how did my grandma & grandad nail my taste so accurately? That's not how it's supposed to work.

It's only now, up here in the loft, seeing all this stuff together, that certain connections & possibilities begin to manifest themselves. What if they'd seen my sister sewing up those garish stage trousers & thought, 'Ah! That's the kind of thing he's into'? & so, when they encountered this shirt in some little Greek street market, they made a beeline for it. The really strange thing is that my grandfather bought one for himself too. He was a former undertaker who ran his own DIY shop. He was a Freemason. He was always building walls or mending or making things. He was possibly the least psychedelic man ever. Why did this shirt appeal to him?

The fact that ideas & artefacts with roots in the experimental art of the 1960s eventually found their way into everyday life in the 1970s Sheffield of my childhood is a source of wonder to me. There's another example opposite:

Is this Op-Art? Boldly contrasting stripes of colour converging on a common vanishing point, giving the illusion of rapid forward movement. A lesser-known work by Bridget Riley maybe? Or Vasarely? An image taken from the catalogue of a cutting-edge Cork Street art gallery?

Nope – it's actually taken from: *The New Indoor Rainbow Vinyl Collection* catalogue – from Crown Wallpapers.

This IS another jumble sale find. I bought it down in London in the early '90s because one of the patterns inside is the one I was surrounded by in my bedroom during my teenage years. I spent hours staring at this wallpaper – putting myself into a self-induced hypnotic state in the process. I'm not sure that was what my mother had in mind when she put the stuff up. I'm guessing she'd read an article in *She* magazine explaining that by surrounding your child with strong visual stimuli, you can spur on mental development. This theory would seem to be backed up by the name given to this particular wallpaper pattern:

'Graduate' – surround your kid with this pulsating graphic design & they'll end up going to university. Guaranteed. What a great idea. A teenage bedroom instantly transformed into a social experiment investigating the effects of environmental factors on learning ability. A very '60s idea.

When I bought this catalogue in the early '90s I had the notion that it could come in useful when I had kids because I'd be able to track down the patterns featured in it & create a stimulating nursery environment of my own. But seeing as my son has just left school & gone into higher education, & this catalogue is still languishing in the loft, I'd say I've missed the boat on that particular ambition. So, although I've enjoyed sharing it with you, *The New Indoor Rainbow Vinyl Collection* catalogue from Crown Wallpapers goes in the 'COB' pile. I'm graduating.

I'd love to be able to claim that this very early live Pulp photo bears witness to our own experiments with the effects of boldly patterned backdrops, this time on a concert-going audience. In reality, it's a picture of me looking a bit glum, performing in front of the flock wallpaper in the upstairs room of the Hallamshire Hotel in Sheffield on Sunday 31 August 1980.

Why am I looking so down? I am sixteen years old. I played my first concert in front of a 'real' (i.e. above school-age) audience just a fortnight ago. This has led to invitations to play more shows. We have been welcomed into the local band scene. I am making lots of new friends. I am drinking in pubs two years before I am legally entitled to do so. Result.

Of course, Pulp didn't break up after The Day That Never Happened. Once the embarrassment faded we began rehearsing again. Then we answered a call in the local newspaper for bands to submit recordings for inclusion on a compilation album called *Bouquet of Steel*. Though we didn't get on the album we did get included in the local bands directory that came with it. That in turn led to us being invited to play at 2 p.m. on a Saturday afternoon at an all-day concert to launch the album at the Leadmill in Sheffield on 16 August 1980. This has since become the official 'birth-date' of Pulp.*

* There's even a plaque on the side of the Leadmill now to commemorate it.

LOCAL BAND
~ FESTIVAL ~

AUG 16   ENTRANCE £1   2-10PM

ARTERY, THE FLYING ALPHONSO BROS.
THE SCARBOROUGH ANTELOPES,
REPULSIVE ALIEN, DIFFICULT DECISION,
THE NAUGHTIEST GIRL WAS A MONITOR,
TREMMERS, CORRIDOR, PULP, STATION 4.

TEA COFFEE SOFT DRINKS + FOOD

THE LEADMILL, LEADMILL RD, SHEFFIELD 1

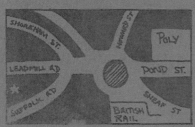

The birth was . . . eventful.

Transport was a problem. Though we didn't have that much equipment there was still too much for us to take on the bus or fit in my mum's car. Luckily my mother was friendly with a guy over the road who sold fruit & veg out of the back of a van. He agreed to deliver us & our gear to the Leadmill on Saturday lunchtime before going on his rounds. So we travelled to our first public appearance sitting on the floor of his van, clasping our instruments whilst cabbages, potatoes & the like rolled around us whenever he turned a corner. When we reached the venue we got some bemused looks from the technical team as we disembarked from a van with 'Mobile Greengrocer's' written in big letters on the side of it. Maybe they thought it was the name of the band.

It turned out we needn't have brought all our gear with us because we were informed that 'the bands are going to use the same backline to save time on change-over'. We nodded our heads in assent – though we didn't have the slightest clue what that meant. We weren't au fait with the jargon yet. We decided it would be safest for us to go & stand at the side of the stage so we couldn't miss our cue to go on.

The Leadmill is an old bus garage & we watched the cavernous space slowly fill up with alternative-looking people who arranged themselves along the back wall of the venue.

Jamie (our usual bass player) was on holiday with his parents so Pip (real name Philip) Thomson, a friend from school, was standing in for him. At almost seventeen I was the oldest member of the band. Dolly had only just turned sixteen. Pip was very slight so, even though he was older than Dolly, he actually looked much younger. About twelve years old. (Pip strongly disagreed with this assessment, saying, 'I must be a MASSIVE twelve-year-old then.') At the other end of the spectrum Jimmy, our drummer, looked & acted like he was thirty-five. He was rumoured to be having an affair with a married woman. Seeing as I didn't even have a steady girlfriend yet this was beyond my comprehension. True to form he travelled to the venue separately from the rest of us & arrived late & half drunk.

This concert was shaping up to be just as stressful & disastrous as the one at school. Under-rehearsed, out of our depth & with an inebriated drummer – all the ingredients were there for another stinker.

Yet I found I wasn't half as nervous as before. We didn't know these people in the audience. We weren't going to have to endure their smirks in the school corridor the next day if it went wrong. If we crashed & burned we could walk away from the wreckage & make like nothing had happened. In the aftermath of the school concert Mr Jarvis the maths teacher had offered me some words of advice that have stayed with me. 'What you've got to remember, Jarvis,' he said, 'is that nobody's heard your songs before. So no one knows if you're playing them right or not.' In other words, nobody knows that you've screwed up unless you let on. Wise words which I'd taken to heart & was determined to put into practice. Forget any ideas about perfection you might have – get up on stage, do the best you can & try to keep a straight face.

By the time it was our turn to play, the venue was about a third full. When I stood at the mic, preparing to start our first song, the nearest audience member was about forty feet away. I said something like, 'You can come a bit closer – we won't bite,' &, to my surprise, one or two people shuffled a few inches nearer. I had harnessed the power of the microphone. This concert was already better than the one at school. & we hadn't even played a note yet.

Seeing as 'Stepping Stone' was the very first song we'd ever played we thought we had that one down pat. We'd even got 'creative' with it: we'd added a dramatic pause in the middle of the song – after the second chorus we all stopped playing & then, starting with the drums, the instruments re-entered one by one, building up to a frantic final chorus & outro. I was really proud of our arrangement. We started the song. It sounded pretty good. Another few audience members edged a little closer to the stage. We were building an atmosphere. We got to the end of the second chorus & the song stopped dead. Perfect. 1, 2, 3, 4 & then . . .

& then nothing. In his drunken state Jimmy thought we'd reached the end of the song already. I turned round & he was smiling at me, glassy-eyed, waiting for the count in to the next number. I was about to point out his mistake when Mr Jarvis's words came back to me: 'No one's heard you before – no one knows if you're playing the songs right or wrong.' I held my tongue. & then I heard an unfamiliar sound coming from behind me. Applause. Yes, not only had no one noticed the mistake, they liked our version of 'Stepping Stone'! Even if it was only about a minute & a half long.

The day's other major blunder was harder to pass off as intentional. We were about to play our epic instrumental 'Message From the Martians' – the one that consisted of the bass line to Joy Division's 'New Dawn Fades' with added sci-fi sound effects – & Pip turned his bass up, as that was the lead instrument in the song. His instrument began to feed back – a low, loud, unpleasant howl of a sound.

Even if you've never been in a band you'll be familiar with feedback. Think of those times you've been on a train & the ticket inspector tries to make an announcement over the tannoy system. 'Travellers in the – whoooo – front two – wheeeeee – sections should . . .' You can see the whole carriage wince as he tries to get to the end of his message amid a hail of electronic distortion. It's like a Death Metal band has hijacked the train. Feedback happens when the microphone can 'hear' itself; in the case of our imaginary ticket inspector, he is holding his microphone too near to one of the speakers.

Back in the Leadmill, Pip was panicking. We had encountered feedback in rehearsals before & we knew the solution was to move away from the speaker. To 'get out of earshot' so to speak. So that's what Pip started to do. He backed away from the bass amplifier.

The feedback continued. He backed off a little more. The feedback continued. He backed off some more.

& then he ran out of stage.

The stage in the Leadmill was only about three feet high (I think it's a little higher now) so he didn't hurt himself. But the fact remained: he fell off stage. In front of about two hundred people. Ouch. His pride was certainly hurt. The audience didn't seem to mind though – as far as they were concerned it was another part of our naive charm. A review of the concert (our first!) from local fanzine *The Bath Banker* captures the mood in the room:

PULP – TEENAGE KICKS RIFF ON 'ACOUSTIC GUITAR BUT DIFFERENT WORDS.
THEY CLAIM TO HAVE WRITTEN 'STEPPING STONE' – IT'S THE DEFINITIVE VERSION!
"SUBTLETY TIME, DEDICATED TO ELVIS" SOUNDS LIKE "DON'T FEAR THE REAPER A BIT.
A DIRGE. "MESSAGE FOR THE MARTIANS" WITH A KEYBOARDIST WHO HADN'T LEARNT
THE OTHER SONGS. ANOTHER DIRGE. THE APPEARANCE OF THE FRONT MAN IS ENTERTAINING.
A FUN SHOW. TUNING UP OF HOPELESSLY OUT OF TUNE SEMI-AC. "HAPPY HOUSE" RIFF OUT
OF TUNE. DIFFERENT WORDS. "I WONT SAY THAT THIS IS THE PENULTIMATE SONG
BECAUSE THAT'S PRETENTIOUS". "THIS IS FOR DANCING BUT I DONT SUPPOSE ANYBODY'S
GOING TO DANCE. SOUNDS LIKE "CHRISTINE" AND IS A DISCO SPOOF. I WONDER WHAT
KEITH STRONG WOULD SAY. VAST CHEERING FOR ENCORE. '

The last line of the review was our favourite: 'VAST CHEERING FOR ENCORE.' The fact that we were accident-prone & so obviously clueless had endeared us to the crowd which, let's face it, was made up mainly of other people in bands or their friends. They'd all suffered the same mishaps & loved the way we soldiered on regardless. Classic underdog story. We had arrived.

Standing in the crowd afterwards, watching the next band, people kept coming up to me & saying how much they'd enjoyed our performance. That felt good. Technically, the show had not been that different to the one we did at school. There had still been plenty of mistakes – what was different was our attitude to them. The previous time I'd almost had a nervous breakdown. This time we had a 'carry-on-regardless' mindset. Shit happens. & that not only defused the situation – it turned the mistakes to our advantage. It made us stick out from the other bands on the bill. The audience remembered the 'hicks from the sticks' who fell off the stage & said sarcastic things in between songs. Another important lesson learnt: attitude is everything.

One of the people who came up to congratulate me also asked

whether we'd like to play another concert the following night at the Hallamshire Hotel, supporting a band called 'B-Troop' (at first, I'd thought he'd said 'Beetroot'). Are you kidding? Of course!

Hold tight, here we go . . .

That concert went well. So here I am a fortnight later back on the Hallamshire stage for a second time. This must be a little later in the show because I have taken my jacket off to reveal another shirt with an interesting pattern. This one isn't so space age: it depicts gun dogs & mallards. This I actually bought new from a shop called 'Flip' during a school trip to London. It's not up here in the loft though – I gave it to my nephew a few years ago. The Hopf guitar has been decorated with magazine cuttings & stickers. My look is developing. The piece of brightly coloured material tied to the mic stand is an off-cut from the trousers my sister ran up for our debut performance. I put it there to remind me not to freak out if things went wrong. It seems it didn't completely work: the write-up in the 'Concert List' in the back of the exercise book* reads, 'Hallamshire with Defective Turtles & Mark Mywords. Freak out on my part. Enjoyable (Tape).'

The 'freak-out' happened when my guitar stopped working in the middle of a song & I couldn't get it to make a noise again, no matter how hard I tried. Finally, in a state of impotent frustration, I lay on my back on the floor in front of the stage & spun around on the ground for a minute or so. Like a little kid having a tantrum. With the silent guitar still hanging around my neck. When I'd finished I lay there embarrassed & wondering what to do next. & then I heard that curious sound again. The sound of people clapping. What? Why were they applauding that? It was tantamount to applauding someone for having an epileptic fit. Sick bastards . . .

Up to that moment I'd stood pretty much stock-still on stage – I was too scared of making a mistake to move. I had

* See page 189.

broken the 'no freak-out' rule – but accidentally learnt yet another important lesson in the process: you can use your body to get your point across. The audience is there to see you as well as hear you. So give them something to look at.

Master of the understatement, I wrote, 'August 1980 = Pulp's most Active month to date' in the exercise book. Like it's a clerical ledger. Yes, statistically speaking we played four concerts in the space of a single month – but more importantly August 1980 was the month Pulp changed from being a schoolboy fantasy into a tangible reality. We are out in the world – making mistakes & learning lessons. Our schooldays are, literally & figuratively, coming to an end. We're almost done with this exercise book, for instance.

We're finally on the launch pad.

1 Meaningless, [illegible]
2 Please Don't Worry
3 What do You Say
4 Wishful Thinking
5 My Girl
6 Test of Affection
7 Refuse to be Blind
8 Crabs that Killed stuff
_____
ENCORE (?)
        SHAKESPEARE Rock

Chapter Sixteen

A lot has been written about the relationship between technology & music.

Rock & Roll couldn't have happened without electric guitars. Acid House relied on the invention of the Roland TB-303 for its signature sound. & the early '80s indie music scene in Sheffield would have been nothing without photocopiers.

Photocopiers democratised the print media. They were the 'punk' moment for publishing. Anyone with a few pence to spare could go to their local corner shop or post office & get something printed. You could get the word out very cheaply.

Our very first review appeared in a photocopied fanzine, *The Bath Banker* – photocopiers allowed an 'underground' press to develop & flourish. The encouragement that press provided was key to our development. Though fanzines had minuscule circulations, & were often barely legible, being included in them was important. Someone had noticed us! That meant we really existed.

But photocopiers truly came into their own, as far as Pulp were concerned, because they were our gateway into the world of flyposting.

There are lots of examples of our involvement in this world up here in the loft. Flyposting was big in post-punk Sheffield. I'd noticed self-printed posters for concerts by The Human League & Cabaret Voltaire on trips into the city centre, but I had been too young to attend the shows they advertised.

When I saw the A4 poster opposite (for our concert supporting The Defective Turtles at the Hallamshire Hotel) pasted on a wall near the 'Impulse' record shop, I was inspired. We could (& should) be doing that ourselves! It was yet another way of us being part of the scene.

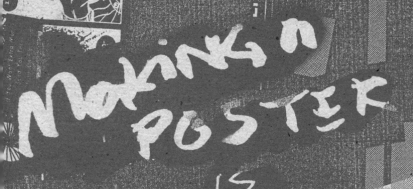

Making a POSTER

IS

FUN & EASY

1 Find a picture you like from an old book or magazine (in my case an illustration of a Plesiosaur from an old encyclopaedia)

2 Add the band logo & some informative text ('there's no substitute for talent'! – another case of 'positive visualisation'?)

3 Go to the photocopy shop. & you're ready to go..

PULP

THERE'S NO SUBSTITUTE FOR TALENT

© 1980 MANTIS INC

Then comes the exciting part –
putting the posters up.
It's exciting because

**FLYPOSTING
IS ILLEGAL**

The four of us met at my house after we'd all had our dinners. I had the posters, which I'd printed in the school library. I'd also mixed up some flour & water in a bucket to act as paste. I found a couple of large paintbrushes in my grandad's garage. We were all set. We walked to the bus stop. We weren't wearing overalls because we thought that would only serve to draw attention to ourselves. We had the paste bucket hidden inside a large carrier bag. It was early September so it was still light when we got off the bus in the centre of town. Sheffield city centre was deserted. There was an eerie silence all around as we walked past the closed shops & office buildings on the way to our first destination – the Hole in the Road.

I loved the Hole in the Road because it looked like a flying saucer that had landed on Earth & was trying to disguise itself as a traffic island. Its real name was Castle Square (confusing, given its shape) & it had walkways leading to it from all the surrounding streets which met in an underground circular area that was open to the sky in its very centre. There was a fish tank set into one of the walls of the central 'hub' & I, like countless other Sheffield kids of my generation, had been kept under control during shopping trips to town with my mum by the promise that I would be allowed to 'go & see the fishes' if I behaved myself. That was in the late 1960s. Now, at the beginning of the '80s, the place had become a dilapidated hangout for winos, & the fish tank had a metal grille over it due to vandalism. It was a very popular flyposting spot though – there was still a lot of 'footfall' due to people using it as a shortcut to get from one part of the city to another.

One of us held the poster in place, another applied the paste & the other two kept a lookout for 'the filth'. We'd unwittingly picked a stressful place to start because there were so many walkways that converged on the central area. A copper might materialise from anywhere. At any moment. & the dome-like structure we were standing under caused a kind of 'Whispering-Gallery-of-St Paul's' audio effect which made it impossible to pinpoint which direction any footsteps were coming from. Tense. Speed was of the essence. Once the poster was on the wall we walked quickly away, affecting as much nonchalance as we were capable of. Maybe one of us even whistled. 'Nothing to see here, officer.'

After 'breaking our duck' we did a tour of all the usual places people put up posters – near venues & record shops – but we also posted a few in special, out-of-the-way locations that I'd made a note of during my wanderings around town. These were really messages to other people in bands: 'Hey, look – there's a new group on the scene, & we're going to places other bands haven't been yet. We're different.' It was a statement of intent. I wanted people to notice we'd arrived.

Sheffield was a ghost town that night. We didn't see a single other human being, let alone a policeman. After the last poster went up we caught the bus home in a state of exhilaration. We'd done it – & we were still free men. Lying in bed at home later I found it difficult to get to sleep. I couldn't wait to go to town at the weekend & see our posters proudly displayed for all the world to see. Our very first public exhibition.

We met up on Saturday morning & went to town en masse. First stop: the Hole in the Road. No posters. Strange.

We retraced our steps. Everywhere it was the same story. Not one poster. Even in our unique, out-of-the-way places. Had a mysterious someone been following us & torn them down? Or perhaps it had been very windy later that night & the posters blew off the walls before they'd had chance to dry? Then the awful truth dawned on me: it was my fault. I'd mixed the flour-&-water paste. I'd never done it before. I didn't know what the correct flour:water ratio was. I'd winged it. & I probably didn't want to get shouted at for using up all the flour in the kitchen cupboard. Thinking back, the mixture had been quite . . . runny. There was no mystery to solve. As soon as the posters dried they had simply slid off the walls & into oblivion. I'd fucked up. All that wasted effort. Sorry, guys.

We didn't give up after that inauspicious start though – I atoned for my mistake by splashing out on some genuine wallpaper paste & we were back in business. & now we really did begin our participation in that long-running, free, outdoor art exhibition that was 'Sheffield Indie Band Posters of the Early 1980s'. (It's only a matter of time until there's a Taschen coffee-table book bearing that name, surely.)

Our designs even got quite sophisticated. The poster on the previous page which dates, from a few years later, features an original illustration by my girlfriend (the one who gave me the Marianne Faithfull record.) The Beehive was a pub on West Street – the same street as the Hallamshire Hotel. Though the pubs were only fifty yards away from each other they were worlds apart. The Beehive was where the more established, first-wave Sheffield bands like Cabaret Voltaire hung out (their rehearsal room/studio Western Works was just round the corner) whereas the Hallamshire was home to younger, up-&-coming bands such as ourselves. Sometimes we would venture up to the Beehive & gaze in awe at The Cabs (as they were known locally) & their friends. They seemed impossibly cool & sophisticated compared to us. We were still underage drinkers, they had written & recorded 'Nag, Nag, Nag', one of the best singles of all time. They knew how to use synthesisers, we'd only just learnt how to mix wallpaper paste.

The poster dates from a few years after those encounters. The Beehive had undergone the indignity of being turned into one of Sheffield's first 'Fun Pubs'. It was now rebranded as Rockwells. The Cabs & their acolytes were long gone. The pub was experimenting with putting on live bands & we got offered a concert. It says 'double set' on the poster because they asked us to play two shows during the course of the night – a first for us. They were offering a fee of £50; plus, admission was free so we could invite as many of our friends as we wanted. Getting paid for a concert was still a rare occurrence back then so we stifled any qualms we may have had about the desecration of a local musical landmark & accepted the booking. I came up with a concept (I still hadn't entirely learnt my lesson): we would play the first set dressed entirely in black & the second clad completely in white. Hence the 'half & half' figure depicted on the poster. When it came down to it, I was the only member of the band who actually brought two outfits. I remember having to get changed in the men's toilets between shows. The glamour of showbiz. We didn't want to play exactly the same set twice in a row so we tried out some new songs & even attempted a cover of 'Hurry Up Harry' by Sham 69. The guys in smart-casual attire at the bar were not impressed. We didn't get invited back.

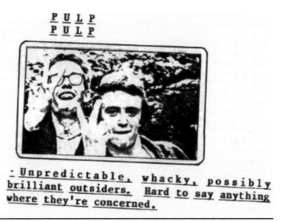

P U L P
P U L P

‗ Unpredictable, whacky, possibly brilliant outsiders. Hard to say anything where they're concerned.

Most of our press coverage was still confined to the photocopied pages of local fanzines. The image above is taken from *NMX* – one of the most long-established. At one time every other person you met at a concert would try to sell you a copy of their home-made fanzine. (The fact that you could often talk your way into a show for free – & thus avoid the astronomical 50p entrance fee – if you said you were going to review it, probably had something to do with this publishing boom.) The photo is of me & our drummer Jimmy. You can see the difference in our temperaments: I'm giving the peace sign, he's telling the photographer to 'fuck off'. Not long after this picture was taken Jimmy did indeed 'fuck off.' He left the band.

Once more the local paper came to our rescue. Shortly before Jimmy's departure we'd taken part in a local bands competition organised by the *Sheffield Star* called 'Search For a Star'. There were to be preliminary heats all over town, followed by a grand finale at the Top Rank theatre in the city centre. First prize was a day in a recording studio. Our heat was in a church hall in Frecheville, a suburb just down the road. The other bands were the usual assortment of heavy metal groups & folkies, apart from one other 'New Wave' band called 'Vector 77'. The singer had highly conditioned hair, swept across his forehead in a quasi-Phil Oakey style, & severe acne. Each band was allowed to play a maximum of three songs & one that stuck in my mind from their audition was a synth-ballad called 'Corner Shop Man'. (Still thinking about stealing that title.) Their drummer caught my eye. He was very petite & wore a mohair jumper. He played super-energetically & had loads of drums in his kit. It was fascinating to watch him do a drum-fill because you were constantly wondering whether he'd ever get to the end of it.

We played after Vector 77 & were the last band in our particular heat. All the bands then lined up whilst the judges gave their appraisal of the evening's performances. When their summary of our short set began with the words 'Loved the energy . . .' I knew we hadn't got through to the next round. Vector 77 didn't get through either. We commiserated together afterwards & swapped phone numbers. I was astounded that there was another 'alternative' band in our part of town. It was such a backwater. All the bands we'd encountered on the scene so far seemed to come from the posher end of Sheffield. When Jimmy jumped ship a few months later I remembered Wayne, Vector 77's diminutive drummer, dug out his number & asked him if he'd like to join our band. He said yes.

The first line-up of Pulp to make it on to the nation's airwaves was now complete. (Cue drum roll.)

Chapter Seventeen

This ticket changed my life.

This is a holy relic.

The reason we're up here is to uncover items like this ticket. It's the ticket that first got us through the front door. & it could so easily have got thrown away. It was in a big pile of waste paper in the far corner of the loft. What we are looking at here is a ticket to the *John Peel Roadshow* at Sheffield Polytechnic.

We had made our first attempt at a professional recording about three weeks before the *John Peel Roadshow* came to town. Since Wayne's arrival in May we had been trying to 'progress'. I'd found out about a guy with a studio in his semi-detached house in Handsworth (another nothing-y suburb within walking distance of home) during a conversation with a bloke from a local band called The Scarborough Antelopes. (There certainly were some good band names around in those days.) The bloke (whose name was Mark) worked on a butcher's stall at the same indoor market I had my Saturday job as an apprentice fishmonger. Sometimes I would go over & have a chat with him during lunch break. Other lunchtimes I would just go & stare at a really attractive girl who worked on the pet-food stall. The studio in Handsworth was incongruously named 'Studio Electrophonique' & was run by a man called Ken Patten. Mark referred to him as 'The Colonel'. I was intrigued. Mark was at great pains to tell me how cheap the studio was. I was even more intrigued. He gave me 'The Colonel's' number. When I got home I rang for a quote – Mark had been true to his word. The Colonel's studio was *very* reasonably priced. Within a month we saved enough money for one day's worth of recording & mixing.

Here we are on our way to the studio. OK, not quite, but this picture was taken around the same time. I love this photo. The Pulp Wardrobe has been made manifest. & in a dystopian, industrial corridor/building site environment to boot. I'm wearing the 'Stargate' shirt I showed you earlier. Dolly is sporting a trilby. Wayne's got a bow tie on. Jamie's shirt has collars that look like a spaniel's ears. Jamie & I have also brought our instruments with us to the photo-shoot. A day out for them. People used to ask us why we played semi-acoustic guitars. Thinking it was a musical or aesthetic choice we'd made. The truth of the matter was that no one wanted those instruments back then because they were deemed old-fashioned. You could pick them up very cheaply (or, in my case, for free). In hindsight I suppose that chimes perfectly with the Pulp ethos: using other people's cast-offs to make something new. Nowadays it's known as 'upcycling'. At the time it was known as 'all we can afford.'

I was very into all those adornments I put on my guitar. That must be why I'm crouching behind my instrument to give it pride of place in the photo. I grew out of this phase not long after but, strangely enough, one of the decorations has survived to this day.

 These doll faces were available in haberdashers' shops. (Perhaps they still are.) They're aimed at people who want to make their own soft toys. Surprisingly big market. If you look closely at the group photo you can see it stuck on my guitar, to the right of the tremolo arm. My bedroom door at home was plastered with stickers & clippings from magazines, so I carried this practice over to my guitar. Nowadays the odd car sticker is the only way I satisfy this compulsive decorative urge. As for this doll face: it *is* adorable & it may seem a little . . . abusive to do so – but it's time to COB it.

Arriving at 32 Handsworth Grange Crescent it was hard to believe this was the fabled 'Studio Electrophonique'. It looked like any other suburban house in the area. Caravan on the drive, pebbledash on the walls. Ken Patten answered the doorbell himself, took us into the kitchen for a cup of tea & quickly laid down the rules of the studio.

1) No shoes indoors (We all dutifully removed our footwear.)
2) No amplifiers (All instruments went straight into his mixing desk.)
3) No drums (Wayne wasn't keen on this one. The Colonel didn't want to get in trouble with his neighbours by making too much noise so he'd invested in a Simmons electronic drumkit. All drummers were to use this instead of their own noisy acoustic kit.)

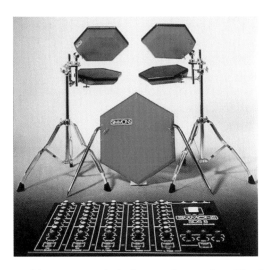

Simmons kits were a relatively new innovation. No drums: just a set of pressure-sensitive pads that triggered electronic approximations of drum sounds. A very '80s instrument. Proud of this piece of cutting-edge technology, the Colonel led us upstairs to show it to us. The kit was in the master bedroom. Even though we'd never been in a recording studio before we knew that this was unusual. The contrast between the space-age drum set, with its geometric-shaped pads & multitude of cables, & the bright pink bedroom suite & matching shag-pile carpet, was something to behold. Whilst this juxtaposition was sinking in he pointed out another technical innovation: because his wife was not too keen on him having musicians in their bedroom unsupervised, he had installed a CCTV camera high in one corner of the room to make sure that nothing untoward went on. OK.

Wayne was left upstairs to acquaint himself with his unfamiliar instrument. (Responsibly.) & the rest of us followed the Colonel back downstairs to the kitchen, where we were shown where to plug in our instruments. Sure enough, on a portable TV next to the toaster, we could see a grainy black-&-white image of Wayne silently going through his drum parts. We were suitably impressed.

Due to all the instruments going through the mixing desk we had to wear headphones in order to play at the same time. It was a novelty to hear ourselves in such detail. A few minor volume adjustments & we were ready. The Colonel pressed 'Record' on his 4-Track tape machine. The tape reels began turning. We were actually, physically 'rolling'. No going back now –

The first time you hear a professional recording of a song you've written really affects you. Up to that point music has been something you've experienced as a 'unified event'. A song feels like a solid object. It comes out of the speaker as a single entity & either you like it or you don't. After you've been in a studio you suddenly become intensely aware of all the constituent parts that make up a musical performance. How turning up the bass drum or the keyboard line, even just a touch, can drastically alter the personality of a whole song. You will never listen to music in the same way again. It's a loss-of-innocence moment. From then on you will constantly be asking yourself what happened in the studio to make the song you are listening to 'work'. What's their secret? How did they do that?

Back in 'Studio Electrophonique', the secret seemed to involve putting lots of echo & reverb on everything. Ken 'Colonel' Patten allowed us to be involved in the mixing of the songs we'd recorded. Fatal error. I had heard my voice on tape before, on our rehearsal cassettes, but this was a new level of clarity. I hated it. Smothering it in echo & reverb made it just about bearable. So I tried it on all the other instruments as well. Result. The Colonel was horrified. It was like I'd done something illegal. He said the recording was too 'wet'. I didn't really know what that meant. I certainly wasn't aware it was a criminal offence. An animated discussion followed. The clock was ticking. A compromise was reached. He dialled back the effects on everything bar the vocal. I guess that meant our recording was now merely 'moist'. I had to admit it sounded better now though. We were good to go. Our first recording session was over.

On the way out of the house he made a point of showing me the caravan at the bottom of his drive & told me that if we ever wanted to make a live recording he had 'mobile facilities'. We shook hands & I said we'd bear that in mind. What a day. What a man.

When I got home I went straight to bed & listened to the cassette of our four songs on the In Tensai Rhythm Machine about fifteen times in a row. I just couldn't believe it. That sound coming out of the speaker was us! It really was. Incredible.

I wanted the whole world to hear it. & soon they would.

Perhaps the stars were aligning: it was only about a week after our debut recording session that there was an announcement in the trusty *Sheffield Star* that none other than John Peel himself was bringing his *Roadshow* to Sheffield Polytechnic as part of a series of concerts for the unemployed. (*Roadshow* makes it sound like there were cancan girls involved but it was essentially just him playing records for a couple of hours.) If I wanted the whole world to hear our demo then here was my chance: the *John Peel Show* comprised the entire musical universe as far as I was concerned.

I went down to the *Roadshow* on my own. I had the cassette of our four songs in my jacket pocket. I had made a cardboard sleeve for it which I'd decorated with some oil pastel crayons I found in a drawer at home. I was pleased with the effect but hadn't realised that the nature of the crayons meant that they never really dried, making the sleeve sticky & prone to smudging. I wrapped it in a sheet of kitchen roll for protection.

I stood in the Phoenix Hall of Sheffield Poly waiting for my moment. I knew better than to approach someone just as they were going on stage. Those last moments before the curtain rises are when performers are at their most vulnerable. You're focusing on the job at hand. Psyching yourself up. Any interruptions or distractions at that time are most unwelcome. Our demo would probably have got launched straight in the bin.

The trouble was, he seemed busy during the whole next two hours as well – cueing up records & searching through his record box for what to play next. It felt wrong to interrupt him. Here I was, standing in the same room as the man who'd been giving me an unparalleled musical education over the past three years. The last thing I wanted to do was to disrespect THE John Peel. But I had to get our tape to him somehow.

I (typically) left it to the last minute. The *Roadshow* came to an end. John Peel started putting his records back into their cases. The crowd began filing out of the hall. In a minute or so everyone would be ushered out of the venue & I would have missed my chance & regret it for ever. That fear forced me to act. I walked towards the stage. As luck would have it, John Peel descended from the podium & walked in my direction at that very same moment. I've often wondered how differently my life would have turned out had he disappeared backstage to his dressing room instead. But he didn't. I intercepted him & awkwardly introduced myself. I got the cassette out of my pocket & unwrapped it. It looked like it was wrapped in toilet paper. The sleeve felt sticky & greasy in my sweaty hand. He had to put down one of his record cases to take it off me. There was a moment of eye contact & then he said that he would listen to the tape on his drive home. With that he was gone. Mission accomplished. Phew.

John Peel was always mentioning on his radio show how many tapes he got given every week. I knew that I shouldn't get my hopes up too high. The important thing, in the short term, was that I'd found the courage to go up to him & give him the tape at all. At least I could rest easy that night knowing I'd done that much.

A week or so later there was a telephone call.

We shared a telephone line with my grandparents who lived next door. My grandfather had done some kind of 'creative' wiring, so the two houses had the same phone number. The upshot of this was that John Peel's producer, Chris Lycett, rang one afternoon & informed my grandmother that he'd like her to come down to the BBC studios in Maida Vale to record a radio session. Being a sharp old bird she realised that the message was probably intended for me. She came round to our house & told me all about it when I got back from school that afternoon.

I know it's a cliché but it really did feel like I'd died & gone to heaven. Can you imagine? John Peel wants US to record a session?! Four schoolkids from Sheffield? I was about to turn eighteen in a week's time – but my birthday present had already arrived. & then some.

If I had to choose the one event that gave me the confidence to devote my life to music this would be it. What a welcome to the adult world.

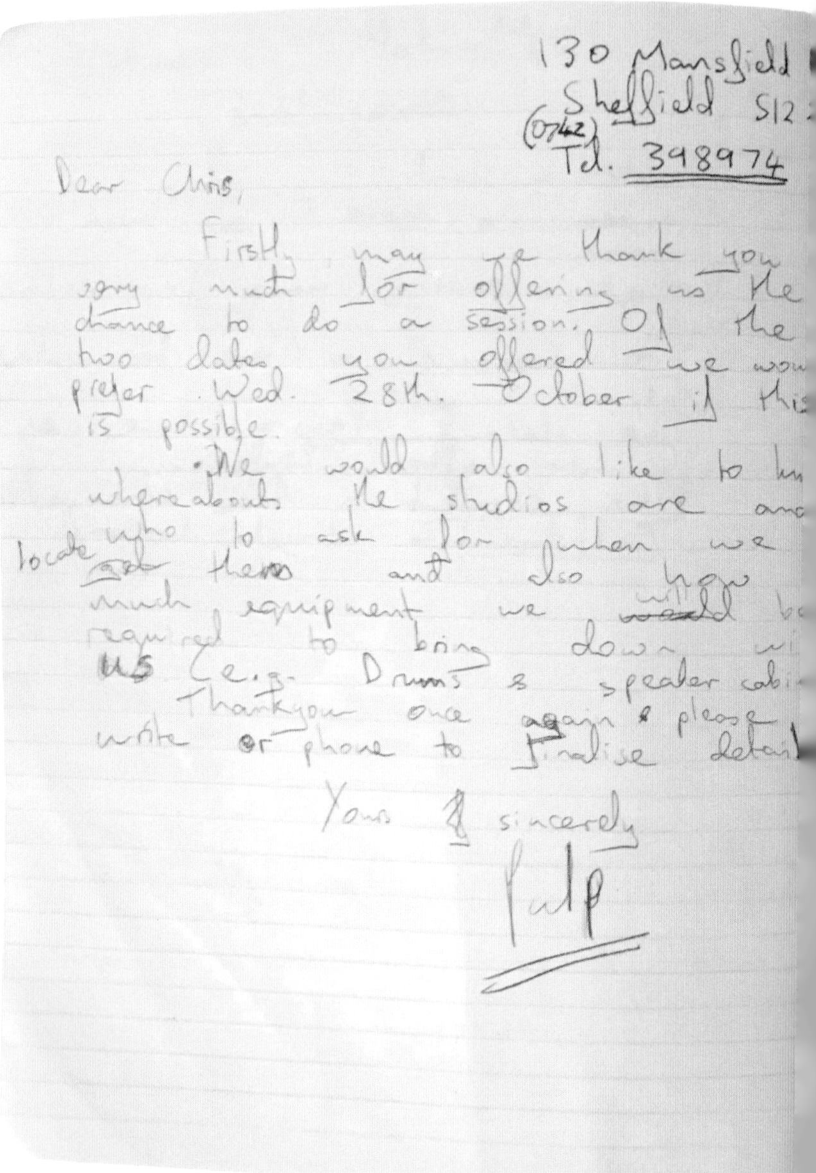

130 Mansfield
Sheffield S12
(0742)
Tel. 398974

Dear Chris,

Firstly, may we thank you
very much for offering us the
chance to do a session. Of the
two dates you offered we woul
prefer Wed. 28th October if this
is possible.

We would also like to kn
whereabouts the studios are and
locate who to ask for when we
get there and also how
much equipment we will be
required to bring down wi
us (e.g. Drums & speaker cabi
Thankyou once again & please
write or phone to finalise detail

Yours sincerely
Pulp

Dear Chris,

We would like some information as regards our impending session.

∴ Date = <u>Wed. 28th October</u>

Could we know :
1) Where?   (drums?)
2) How much equipment?
3) Who to ask <u>for</u>?

Ta

<u>Pulp</u>

Pulpy Pul

U L P

I tried to respond to this awe-inspiring invitation in the most grown-up manner I was capable of. On the previous pages are two drafts of a letter to John Peel's producer. I was obviously trying to find the right 'tone'. Draft 1 is a little formal: 'Firstly, may we thank you very much for offering us the chance to do a session . . . We would also like to know whereabouts the studios are & who to ask for when we locate them'. The reference to 'speaker cabinets' kills me: it's like it really was my grandmother who got invited down to London to do some recording.

Draft 2 tries to affect a more casual approach, as if we get asked to do this kind of thing all the time: 'Could we know: 1) Where? 2) How much equipment? 3) Who to ask for?' It's even signed 'Ta' rather than 'Yours sincerely' as in the previous draft. I wonder which one got sent? As long as we didn't sign it 'Pulpy Pulp' (see Draft 2) I guess it doesn't make much difference. The end result was: on 7 November 1981 Pulp travelled down to London & recorded four songs to be broadcast nationally as part of the *John Peel Show* on BBC Radio 1.

To have found that ticket up here in the loft was like finding a piece of treasure. But the point is that it was *buried* treasure – it's been buried deep within these piles of absolute garbage for years. What was I thinking? KEEP (that's a no-brainer) but for God's sake get it framed or something! It's precious. That ticket commemorates the day the dream came true.

Peel session for city band

SHEFFIELD band Pulp — whose four members are all still at school — have been chosen to record a session for John Peel's prestigious Radio One show.

The band gave Peel — a tape of their music when he appeared at the Polytechnic during the recent concerts for the unemployed.

One phone call later from Peel's producer and Pulp were booked in to record a session in London in November.

Pulp — Jarvis Cocker, aged 18, on guitar and vocals, Peter Dalton, 17, synth / guitar / backing vocals, Jamie Pinchbeck, 17, bass, who all go to City School, and drummer Wayne Furniss,

15, who goes to Frecheville, have only just started to aspire to topping the bill on Sheffield's pub venue circuit.

So it will be quite a leap in status when they are featured on the radio — but other Sheffield bands such as The Comsat Angels and Artery have found out how well a Peel session can work for them.

PAPERBACK

★ **Roman Britain 55BC-AD400** by Malcolm Todd (Fontana History of England, £2.95). Highly readable study of Britain under the Romans — from the conquest of the first century AD. The author draws on archaeological as well as historical evidence.

Interlude 02

If this was a rock biopic the story would end now. Four lads from the North realise their teenage fantasy of pop stardom. The Disney Channel would be all over it. But, in reality, we're only just getting started.

You're about to see a picture of us just before going down to London to record our John Peel session. The source is once again the *Sheffield Star*. The news that four unknown local schoolboys had secured a spot on a national radio station was A Story. A photographer from the newspaper came round to my mum's house. & he had a concept. He wanted one photo of us in our 'stage gear' & then another of us in our school uniforms on the way to school. Even at our tender age we knew that this

idea was cheesy as hell & so, despite the fact that it was our most substantial piece of press so far, we rejected it. This photo was the compromise.

We're standing in the living room we rehearse in every Friday night. Dolly is persevering with his trilby look, Wayne is also sporting another of his signature bow ties, Jamie's collars are far more erect than the last time we saw them & I am pretty much wearing my school uniform – minus the blazer. But, given the subsequent path my life has taken, it's the object that I'm holding up in front of my chest that most catches my eye in this photograph. It's a tortoise.

How, I ask myself, could I possibly have known all those years ago that I was destined for life in the slow lane?

By that, I don't mean that my life has been lacking in incident or interest – or even success – it's just that it has always taken so long for any of these things to happen. When Pulp finally had a hit record in 1995 (fourteen years after this photograph was taken) journalists were fascinated by this extended gap in my biography. What could I possibly have been doing in the interim? Pulp also hold the record for the longest gap between sessions on the *John Peel Show*. The first was broadcast on 18 November 1981, the second followed on 5 March 1993. Radio silence for eleven & a half years.

My working processes are also on the slow side. When mixing the final song on the last album I was involved in (*Beyond the Pale* by JARV IS ... released in 2020) I realised that I'd started work on that particular song eight years previously. Two Olympics ago! When I'm in a good mood I tell myself, 'Creativity is a natural process & you have to allow experiences to percolate through your consciousness before they can form themselves into a piece of work.' When I'm in a bad mood I just say to myself, 'Jarvis, why are you so bloody slooooooow?'

It also extends to my personal life. My partner & I were in a restaurant a few years ago & I spotted the comedian Ronnie

Corbett at another table. She couldn't contain her excitement & turned round to look. As she did so her hair passed over the candle in the middle of our table & set on fire. By the time I was opening my mouth to shout a warning, the man on the table next to us had already thrown a glass of water over my partner's head, immediately extinguishing the flames. We were very grateful & no injuries were sustained but she was, quite naturally, a little upset that it had been left to a complete stranger to save her from going up in smoke whilst I sat there inert. It's a wonder we're still together really. 'What's your problem?' she wanted to know.

It's a valid question. But one I have no answer for, except a rather weak 'It's just the way I am'. As we discussed earlier in the book some people are hares & some are tortoises. I'm not keen on being a slowcoach – but I have come to accept it as an inescapable aspect of my personality.

The trick in life is to turn character defects to your advantage. To make them work for you rather than against you. Otherwise you're screwed (& single). I hope we've gained some practical insight into how this process might work during our 'excavation' of the loft space. This loft is my problem (not the only one – but a significant one nonetheless). This random assortment of objects, festering away in the dark, has weighed on my mind for years. I carried on throwing stuff in here over the course of two decades. I should have dealt with it all years ago & yet here I am only just getting round to it. And there's so much of it. It makes me think of that thing they found in the London sewers a few years back – THE FATBERG!

Those of you with a delicate sensibility might want to skip this paragraph. Fatbergs are formed when fat, oil & grease are poured down sinks & drains & then combine with items that shouldn't be flushed down the toilet, such as wet wipes, cotton buds & disposable nappies. Yuck. The one I'm thinking of was discovered in the sewers of Greenwich in 2019. It weighed 40 tonnes, was the size of a double-decker bus & took up 80 per cent of the sewer's capacity. We assume that when we pour something down the drain or flush it down the toilet that's the end of it – like I thought I was getting rid of things by piling them into this loft – but it isn't. Carry on doing it for long enough, with no thought for the consequences, & you will end up with a problem. A big problem.

OK – now wash your hands.

Opening up this loft has opened a window on to my creative process (as repulsive as that may sound, given what we've just been discussing). In fact, without wishing to get too dramatic about it, I've come to think that this loft, & the objects in it, form a pretty accurate representation of the contents of my brain.

No, don't laugh – just consider it for a moment: think of these objects as not just the accumulated debris of a lifetime but as thoughts & memories. The thoughts & memories we carry with us & which we combine at will to form the narrative we call our 'life story'. So far, I hope that I have done a reasonable job of using what we've unearthed up here to paint a fairly coherent picture of how I got started as a musician. But shuffled in a different order these objects could tell a completely different story. Or no story at all. I had to choose the sequence in which to show them to you. That's creativity. & it takes time.

Life is random – but my, how we love stories. We desperately want it all to make sense. So we put things together in such a way that they appear to do just that. So they tell us a story. It's like seeing faces in clouds or the outlines of mythical figures in the night sky. We see those things because we want to see them. We project a meaning or shape or significance on to our immediate surroundings because it makes us feel better. & we can use anything to get our 'meaning fix'. Even a plastic tortoise . . .

Make no mistake: this is no ordinary plastic tortoise. (It's an AM/FM radio & its eyes glow red & flash in time with the music when you turn it on, for a start.) It's also a powerful personal totem, a symbol of my tendency to take a long time to get around to things. For me, it's both a piece of tat & a sacred object AT THE SAME TIME.

I say that with conviction because I really *am* holding this tortoise in that photograph taken in our living room back in 1981. I haven't Photoshopped it in. I'm standing there on the cusp of entering a new phase of life. Of realising my most heartfelt ambition. & I *will* realise that ambition. But not in the way that I imagine at this particular moment, surrounded by my bandmates & school friends. I have no idea what life's got in store for me. How could I have? But the fact that I've got this plastic tortoise clutched to my chest as though somewhere, somehow I instinctively know that it's going to be a long, long slog, brings a tear to my eye.

It took three weeks for workers using high-power water jets to get rid of that fatberg in Greenwich – but now a fragment of it is on display in the Museum of London (book your tickets). Dare I hope a similar alchemy might be taking place here in the loft? That we are transmuting . . . how can I put it . . . ? That we are transmuting 'base matter' into gold. That's the polite way of saying it. Let's get back to work.

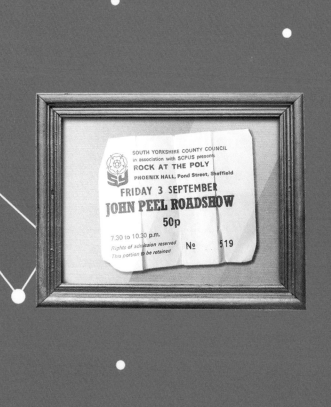

TONARR
DAMP, STINK OF FISH, ONIONS,
UPHOLSTERY, SOMETHING OVERDONE.
CRAMPED, ACHING TO 108°
GREASE FACE HAIR
NO WARM TAP
NO SUNNY CORNER
BEDS
LAID IN VELOUR ACROSS
WITH VELOUR ACROSS
TABLES, BUT IT
WON'T STOP, DOESN'T
MATTER IF YOU SHUT
YOUR EYES BECAUSE
YOU CAN'T SEE ANY
THING ANYWAY. IF
SOMEONE PRISES
A MASK FROM
WHOLE PLACE
WILL GO UP.
(STINK), TIGHT
DAMP CLOTHES,
COLD FEET, NO
SLEEP CAN'T
SLEEP. TRYING
THROUGH
BREATH FINGERNAILS
BLACK HANDS
SHINY TO WIPE THEM.

WHY IS THIS AS THE BIG HIGHWAYS HOWEVER FRIDAY YES THAT
LIGHT JUST CHAIR STOP LOOKIN IN THE BACKGROUND
40 M.P.H IS THAT A BEAT BAND IN STUFF CROWDED
IT'S ALL WHITE, FOOTLIGHTS YOUR SHOOT
LIGHT. ROLL OVER ON TO THE TARCOM
WAIT FOR THE TARCOM

NOT TO
MY NOSE
BROWN
NOWHERE
THIS WAS YOU
BEST SUIT WHEN
YOU CAME IN
WEEKS
YEAR. 16
WITH THE SAME
SHIRT ON THAT'S
CITY DIRT FANNY
CONSTANTLY WORRYING
PISS BUT CAN'T
IS IN YOUR HAND, KEEP SOME FOR

POSTAGE
PAID
PHO 315

Chapter Eighteen

After I left school, writing songs became my full-time job.

It is ironic, to say the least, that I have scribbled the words to a song called 'Tunnel' on the envelope that my most recent dole cheque came in. It's now 1985 & my songwriting career is not going incredibly well. Just as 'Being a Pop Star' wasn't on the School Curriculum, it's not an option down the Job Centre. KEEP.

'Damp, stink of fish, onions, vegetation, something overdone. Cramped aching joints, greasy face – hair. No warmth. No soft corner. Laid in heaps with vague acquaintances ... black fingernails, brown, slimy hands. Nowhere to wipe them. This was your best suit when you came in here. Sixteen weeks with the same shirt on . . .' On second thoughts, perhaps this should go in the COB pile. It's downright depressing. I feel dirty just touching it. It's certainly a far cry from the childish innocence of 'Shakespeare Rock'. What happened?

Well, let's rewind a little: the John Peel session does not lead to fame & fortune. It is broadcast a couple of times & then . . . That's that. The only record company interest we get is from an independent label called Statik which is putting a compilation album together. They can't afford to pay for any studio time so we give them one of the songs from our Ken Patten demo. The album's title is *Your Secret's Safe With Us* – which turns out to be remarkably accurate. Another disappointment.

When school comes to an end the rest of the band go off to university but I'm not ready to give up on the dream just yet. Another line-up of Pulp forms. We make a record called *It* but, again, not many people notice. All this time I've been deferring a place to go & study English Literature at Liverpool University but now the English Department tells me I must take up my place this coming September or they will withdraw the offer. I've decided that I'm going to give the group one more go. No life of academia for me. The safety net has gone. Some nights I wonder whether I've made the right decision. The night I wrote those lyrics on my dole cheque envelope obviously being one of them.

Here's a photograph taken around the same time. I think you can get something of the prevailing atmosphere from this picture.

PULP

Since leaving home I've been living with a friend called Tim in an old factory building in the centre of Sheffield. Tim is the caretaker so we have a rent-free flat on the top floor. That sounds swish but the building was never intended for human habitation & has no heating. In the previous photo I'm standing in an empty unit which has previously been used as a table tennis club, a vegan food co-op (which had to be closed due to a rat infestation) & will soon become home to the Forced Entertainment theatre company. Pulp also recorded some demos here – but, despite the fact that I'm holding a guitar, I don't think this photo was taken during those sessions. I am standing alone in the looming darkness. The floorboards are bare. It's a harsh, spartan environment. The trusty Hopf guitar, held like a shield between me & the world, has been stripped of all its ornamentation. These are cold, hard times. There's a miners' strike taking place at the moment that will change the whole personality of the UK. There are two million people on the dole. Sheffield is particularly hard hit because it is an industrial city. Steel City, even. Welcome to the mid-1980s.

It's not all bad though . . .

Whilst my former bandmates are at real 'uni' I have been attending Disco University. There is a club in Sheffield called The Limit. The Limit is in a basement & it is the only club in town that plays alternative music & where you don't get beaten up if you look a bit different. The toilets are unbelievably disgusting. (You can't have everything.) This is the environment in which the next stage of my musical education will take place. With the pass shown opposite you can get in free all night on a Wednesday & before 10 o'clock on a Monday. (Useful, seeing as I am living on £30 a week.) I never miss a lecture at Disco University – & then do another three years Post Grad for good measure. (Ending up with a Master's in Disco Studies at the end of it?) This here's my social life for that whole six years. KEEP.

At the time of writing, nightclubs are dying out – the number of UK discos has almost halved in the last decade. In 2005 there were 3,144 discos in Britain but this is now down to 1,733. & apparently, this is a worldwide phenomenon.

I'm disturbed by this news because I learnt so much from my time in nightclubs. I would like that resource to be there for future generations. The Limit nightclub was where I learnt what music does to the human body – where I began to learn about the physical side of music. I'd started moving around a little on stage when we played concerts but listening to music was still mainly a head-based, passive experience. Now the rest of me got involved. I guess what I'm trying to say is: The Limit is where I learnt how to dance.

never thought of myself as much of a disco dancer. Occasionally there had been sponsored dances at school (a way of raising money for charity) but they were more about copping off than dancing. My sister had started going to The Limit with some friends from school & I felt jealous about her getting into nightlife before me, seeing as she was two years younger. I could justify my presence by pretending that I was looking out for her.

The sound system in The Limit wasn't exactly hi-fi but it was loud – & most importantly, it had bass. Of course, I'd heard bass before (remember the unfortunate incident involving feedback during our concert at the Leadmill?). But this was bass on another level. This was a sound you could actually feel in your body. After the tinny transistor radio I'd grown up with, discovering bass was like discovering a whole new musical continent. &, consequently, a whole new way of reacting to music – dancing.

Dancing didn't come naturally to me. There was the self-consciousness barrier to get over. Think of times you've been at a wedding. The bride & groom have their first dance & then the other guests move on the floor to join them. Everyone is a little awkward & stiff at first. They need to get warmed up. It was the same for me in The Limit: your first dance is always a bit excruciating because you think, 'Oh, everyone's looking at me,' or, 'Do people move their arms when dancing or do they keep them by their sides?' You're thinking about the act of dancing rather than actually doing it. But hopefully, after one or two records, you get into it & then all of a sudden you're moving without thinking about it any more. You might even find you're waving your hands in the air. & you never consciously thought 'Oh my God, I'm going to put my hand in the air!' Your hand is waving in the air almost of its own volition. It just happened.

There was a general feeling at the time that dance music wasn't 'real'. That it wasn't serious enough. They called disco music 'mindless boogie' – as if that was some sort of insult! Well, it isn't – that's the beauty of dancing to music in a club. You switch off your mind & your body takes over. It's a form of meditation if you think about it. Actually – don't think about it (that would be defeating the object): FEEL it. FEEL the bass travelling through your body & telling you how & when to move. The human brain has been put in its proper place: on an equal footing with the other major organs. It's no longer bossing everyone else around. All on a level playing field. Or preferably, a level dance floor. We move as one. & we can now discover a new version of ourselves: the Night Version.

As I say, I'd never really thought of myself as a 'Nightclub Person' but once I took the plunge I loved this brand-new way of reacting to music. Plus, in the years I was going to The Limit every week, dancing was probably the only physical exercise I ever got.

The structure of a night at The Limit never varied. The DJ played more or less the same records every single night. An astounding statistic when you consider that I went to The Limit at least once a week between the years of 1982 & 1988. Very Zen. It was like being at some austere mountain retreat in the Himalayas. But, rather than being summoned to prayer two hours before dawn by the sound of a gong, at 10 p.m. sharp the DJ would say, 'Hi, I'm Paul Lincoln, welcome to The Limit Club, starting off tonight with . . .' & the ceremony would begin. 'Planet Claire' by the B-52's was his favoured opening track, then, at various points in the evening, you'd get 'The Passenger' by Iggy Pop, 'Sex Machine' by James Brown, 'Shack Up' by A Certain Ratio. Apart from his inscrutable intro he didn't talk much between the records. His other most significant utterance being, 'Steve to the wine bar,' which came at sporadic intervals throughout the evening. I always thought this must be some kind of coded message but quite what it signified I never found out. (Stop over-thinking things . . .)

'Bela Lugosi's Dead' by Bauhaus went on around midnight (of course!) – I know every single second of that record (& many others) off by heart without ever having owned it because I heard it so many times over the years on The Limit dance floor. I never got tired of dancing to it, though. (&, before you ask – no, I was never a goth.) The way the echoes of the rimshots on the snare drum bounce around you, giving so many options for rhythms to lock on to. You can raise one shoulder in time (a personal favourite). You can take one step forward & one step back whilst staring at the floor (the favoured dance of goths at the time). &, underneath all that complex rhythmic activity, the stupendous simplicity of David J's three-note bass line making sure you never lose your bearings.

Actually, I claim to be familiar with every second of 'Bela Lugosi's Dead' but it would appear that's not entirely true: I always assumed that Pete Murphy is singing, 'I'm dead, I'm dead, I'm dead,' towards the end of the song but a visit to a particularly adventurous karaoke bar recently informed me that the official lyric is, 'Undead, undead, undead.' I much prefer my version. In The Limit, reaching that point of the song made me think of the 'Turn off your mind, relax & float downstream. It is not dying' line from The Beatles' 'Tomorrow Never Knows'. Ego death on the dance floor. Regression back to an older, more primitive way of being. A state of bliss & non-being where the mysterious Steve is constantly, endlessly on his way to the wine bar.

A few years ago I was asked to contribute to a special edition of a magazine that was dedicated to the subject of 'Nightlife' & my mind immediately went back to those nights I spent in The Limit. The first place I discovered the 'Night Version' of myself. Here's what I wrote:

Would you like to hear a story?

There was once a nightclub that was free to get into before 10pm. & you'd get a buzzy eardrum from someone trying to tell you something really earnest & dead interesting – philosophical even – but maybe a bit inappropriate seeing as 'Human Fly' is playing in the background & you're into the subject & everything but they're shouting so loud to try & make their point that it actually hurts. So you make your excuses & then split & in a way that walk home is your favourite bit because nobody else lives in that industrial area & the buildings are tall & massive against the brownish sky like a film set they forgot to strike down & now you are the main character in this movie & now you call the shots & conjure whatever you want out of this darkness. The darkness all around & the darkness within you. The dark corners of yourself that you haven't had time to explore yet. & in the day it's very hard to feel like the master of anything but here in the nighttime it's your time in the lime-light. Or the lamp-light. No difference really – you own this town. You are a city & you feel life – the Night-Life – move through you & in YouCity night goes on as long as you want it to because you're

in control & unsanctioned daybreak is illegal & there's
plenty more where that came from . . .
What if there was a person like that?
****

How do we show our true colours?
How do we display ourselves to our best advantage?

Contrast.
By standing against a dark background
So we show up nice & bright
Like jewellery on a velvet cushion.
In full effect against the fathomless void.

'In full effect against the fathomless void' – that's what's really
happening in that photograph at the beginning of this chapter.
I'm making a valiant stand against the forces of darkness. I'm
going to tough it out. Take it like a man. I'm going to find my
way out of The Tunnel.

What happened to me after I left school? Life happened.

ICA
Supermarket
STORUMAN

Chapter Nineteen

You are looking at the jewel in the crown of my carrier bag collection.

.

The carrier bag collection started accidentally – as my jumble sale habit grew, so did my collection. Sometimes a carrier would feature a design I really liked & so I would use that as my 'briefcase' for that particular week.*

This particular beauty is from a supermarket within the Arctic Circle. That explains the two reindeer grazing beneath the midnight sun featured on it. It dates from the early 2000s. I'm still always on the lookout for a good carrier bag no matter where I am in the world. They're harder to find now that reusable tote bags have become so ubiquitous but I persevere. KEEP (or recycle).

I mention that my jumble sale habit escalated after I left home. This was both logical – I now had to buy all my clothes & homewares myself – & essential – I still had hardly any money. I still had hardly any money because I was on the dole.

(To be precise I was on Supplementary Benefit – 'the dole' just sounds more . . . iconic.) This meant that every fortnight I went to the dole office, presented the form pictured opposite, & signed on. Two days later a green giro cheque would arrive in a brown envelope (like the one we found earlier with lyrics scribbled all over it). I would then cash my giro at the post office & live on that money for the next two weeks. As I said before, that worked out at about £30 per week. This was the lifestyle of just about every member of a Sheffield band that I knew in the early 1980s.

I'd been told by older members of bands we'd played concerts with that you could sign on straight after leaving school. So that's exactly what I did. 'From sixth form to the scrapheap,' as my mum put it. It didn't feel like that though – now I would have all my days free to write songs & generally be creative. &, given that my income up to this point had been a Saturday job in the fish market that paid £15, I was actually getting a raise! Come on!

Depending on your political persuasion you will now be

* It's a habit that's stuck: I went round to a friend's house the other day & the first thing he said upon opening the door was, 'Have you left your carrier on the train?'

NEFIT ATTENDANCE CARD

INITIALS	NI NUMBER
JB.	63 C

AIMING BENEFIT

ployment benefit
you are
ent Benefit Office
right Please bring

u could lose
ct day, go to the
ext day you can

if you claim
card and put it in
f you become
on your first day

dvice

BOX	TIME
21	10.45

YOU SHOULD ATTEND

ON 24.4.84.
THEN NEXT ON

AND THEN EVERY
SECOND WEEK ON

TUES DAY

2 WHEN YOU STOP CLAIMING

Please sign and return this form on your last day of unemployment

Below, fill in the dates from the day you last signed at the Unemployment Benefit Office to your
last day of unemployment

I HAVE READ AND UNDERSTAND the leaflet 'Responsibilities of Claimants' (UBL 18)

I DECLARE that on the following dates.

I was unemployed and did no work. I was able and willing to do any suitable work but was unabl
to get any, my circumstances and those of my dependants were as last stated (if there was
change cross out this last item), and I CLAIM BENEFIT for those dates included above for which I
have not already claimed in advance

Date

Signature

We may have paid you in advance for all or some of the dates you have entered above.
We will pay any outstanding unemployment benefit by post to your home address on return of
this card with parts 2 and 3 completed

thinking either 'lucky bastard!' or 'social security scrounger'. Both responses are valid. I'm just trying to paint an accurate picture of how things were back in the day, officer. But one thing's for sure: it's an option that no longer exists today. Supplementary benefit was scrapped in 1988. To explain how & why that happened we are going to have to address a particular elephant in the room.

Or should that be 'elephant in the bag'? A clutch bag this time rather than a carrier bag. What could it contain? Let's study it: it's a printed cardboard representation of a blue leather clutch bag. The colour is a clue – as is the green sticker in the left-hand corner that reads 'Election Bargain! £3.50 [crossed out] £1.95'. There's a political dimension to this clutch bag. Allow me to open it.

The bag contains a pamphlet & other printed matter. One of the printed items is a colour-in paper doll kit – the type where you first colour & cut out the doll & then do the same with various outfits & accessories. I want to draw your attention to the cut-out hairstyle – surely that's a giveaway? No? OK – in that case I guess it's time for the big reveal:

'The Thatcher Bag is full of tricks' – what we are looking at here is a cardboard facsimile of Margaret Thatcher's handbag. Aaargh!

You may be surprised to learn that I have such an item in my possession. I'm a leftie – M*rg*ret Hild* Th*tcher is a kind of Folk Devil for people like me. Explain yourself, Cocker!

Well, I bought this from WHSmith's in 1979. There was a table on the first floor of the shop where they sold remaindered books very cheaply. I got some good things from that table: an

English translation of Serge Gainsbourg's *Yevgeni Sokolov*, a 'novelisation' of Brian De Palma's *Phantom of the Paradise*, a weird illustrated sci-fi novel by Brian Aldiss called *Brothers of the Head* (just trying to claw back some credibility here) & this – published in 1978 by Quartet Books. All these books would have been priced somewhere between 50p & £1.

There's a lesson to be learnt here. I hardly knew who Margaret Thatcher was at the time I bought this. I was fifteen years old. I was aware that politics existed but didn't feel they directly affected my life. Politics was something that older people read up on in newspapers & then complained about in pubs. I certainly could not have known in advance the devastating effect this woman was going to have on the country in general & my home town in particular. So why did I buy the Thatcher Bag? There must have been another factor in my decision besides its cheapness. I think it's because I saw it as a 'pop' item.

Specifically, it reminded me of this 'pop' item – the insert that came in the other half of the gatefold sleeve of The Beatles' *Sgt. Pepper's Lonely Hearts Club Band*. Designed by famous pop artist Peter Blake in 1967. This cardboard insert features five Sgt. Pepper cut-outs: a moustache, a postcard, uniform stripes, badges & a 'stand-up' depicting the band themselves. This insert was a mythical object in our house when I was a kid. Because we had the album in our record rack but the insert was missing.* I knew it existed though – I'd seen it with my own eyes when I went round to my Aunty Mandy's house & looked through her record collection. I was beyond jealous. I kept looking in the empty pocket of our *Sgt. Pepper* record sleeve as if I expected it to magically materialise. (I was around eleven years old at the time.) I quizzed my mum on its whereabouts. I looked through all the other record sleeves in our rack to check that it hadn't got put in one of them by mistake. At one point I even mused as to whether my father had taken it with him when he left home. I was obsessed.

Of course, I'm not the only member of my generation to grow up with a Beatles obsession – No Beatles, no Br*tp*p. How could I have failed to be obsessed with them? 'She Loves You' was Number 1 in the charts on the day I was born. My dad left home in 1970, the same year they split up. In between those two dates they were a shadowy, benevolent presence in my life. I was too young to have consciously been into them – but I had FELT them nonetheless. Perhaps that made the spell they cast over me even stronger.

In the mid-'70s, when I got my first radio cassette recorder (a less snazzy precursor to the In Tensai Rhythm Machine) I would stay in during the school holidays listening to the local radio station, hoping they'd play a Beatles song I hadn't heard before so I could tape it. I first heard 'Hey Jude' & 'Birthday' from the *White Album* using this method. Time-consuming – but very satisfying when I 'bagged' a new song.

* This photo is of the insert from a copy of the record I bought many years later.

Even more books have been written about The Beatles than the 'Punk Explosion' so I'm not going to dwell on them for too long but . . .

Looking back at that 'Pulp Master Plan' in my exercise book, the idea of 'Mantis Inc.' – the record label/radio station/ TV network that is going to benevolently emancipate 'repressed artists' & bring culture to the masses – is a blatant rip-off of what The Beatles had tried to do with 'Apple Corps' – their attempt to wrestle control of the means of production back from the Establishment. (A 'Western form of Communism' as Paul McCartney put it in an interview at the time.) I could never have come up with an idea like that on my own.

They were an inspiration – especially to people from a lower-class background. The fact that 'four ordinary lads from the 'Pool' became the biggest band in the world ever was . . . encouraging. Pop culture couldn't just equal the achievements of 'official' culture – it could piss all over them.

I'll stop gushing now. I may not have named any of my kids after members of The Beatles but I think you can tell I'm a fan. For me they are the ultimate example of Good Pop.

The Thatcher Bag, however, for me heralds the beginning of the era of 'Bad Pop'. Though it was intended as a satirical item – something designed to make fun of this new force on the political stage – it inadvertently bears witness to a profound change in British public life. Because from now on politicians are going to use the tools & gimmicks of Pop to get their message across. They are going to employ advertising agencies & 'creatives' to invent their new Pop: a Pop that now stands for 'Populism' rather than 'Popular'. This Pop is no longer a self-generated art form for the masses – but it will use the same tropes & techniques that made Good Pop work in order to manipulate the public's behaviour. (Boo.)

But I bought it – literally. I opened up the Thatcher Bag on the top floor of WHSmith's & I thought, 'Ooh, that's a fun item! Something a bit different.' & I took it to the till & purchased it.

Terribly embarrassing to still have it in my possession now, of course. COB – no question. (Although I just looked online & saw one offered for sale for £325 so perhaps we have to invent a new category: SELL ON EBAY. 'The market is never wrong' & all that . . .)

Let's carry on. Another carrier from the collection. Good size. Strong handles. Not a tribute to the late, great Christopher – author of *God is Not Great* & *Hitch-22*. The sight of this carrier bag will strike fear into the hearts of Sheffielders of a certain age. Hitchens was a shop on Attercliffe Road in Sheffield & I've introduced this bag into the narrative at this point to give the lie to this idea that 'the market is always right'. Hitchens sold items which had been featured in mail-order catalogues & failed to sell. They had been offered for sale on the free market & the public had turned their noses up at them. & now they were here.

Think of it as a proto-TK Maxx – or, better still, a hybrid of TK Maxx & Argos. (I'm making it sound much more exciting than it was.)

God, I hated being made to trail along to Hitchens with my mother. Even at a young age I could sense the desperate, depressing atmosphere of the place.

There was a reason the stuff in Hitchens was cheap: it was crap. But crap with a logo on it. 'Freedom of choice' may be the mantra of the market but, if all you've got to choose from is rubbish, what kind of choice is that? That's another reason I was lucky to discover jumble sales when I did. Although people often found the clothes I wore a source of amusement, at least I was getting the chance to do my own thing – rather than meekly trying (& failing) to join in. COB.

I looked at what was on offer to a person on the dole in the early '80s & I decided that the stuff people were throwing away was far better. & it wasn't just clothes. I was discovering books, magazines, records . . .

A case in point: I read Federico Fellini's masterpiece *La Dolce Vita* long before I got a chance to see it. I got this 'Book of the Film' from a sale that was held every other Tuesday at the Royal Institute for the Blind. The sale took place under the stage in the function room. To get to it you had to go through a trapdoor & then descend a very steep ladder. You were taking your life in your hands every time you went down there. (I guess it was even harder if you were actually blind.) The sense of adventure was another major part of the appeal of the Jumble Life.

It's easy to forget that there was once a time when books went out of print, films disappeared from cinemas & records got deleted. Stuff got forgotten. We're so used to everything being available all the time, any time, today. Choosing has become more of a problem than finding. But back in the early '80s this book was the only way for me to experience *La Dolce Vita*. I obviously wasn't getting the full picture – but it was better than nothing. I had made contact with another great work of art.

Though I didn't know it at the time, by going to jumble sales I was able to benefit from a publishing boom in the twentieth century that had started with Penguin Books & continued through other publishers such as Paul Hamlyn – publishers whose mission was to bring quality art and literature to the masses. To 'democratise' culture, if you like. Another major example of 'Good Pop'. The fact that these books then ended up in jumble sales might suggest that this initiative failed – but, if so, society's loss turned out to be my gain. I knew that if I searched hard enough I could unearth the information & inspiration I needed to survive Th*tcher's Britain. Relics from a better way of life. It was all there, waiting to be found. The Sweet Life indeed.

It was intoxicating. Soon carrier bags weren't enough. I graduated to bin bags. That was when this collection of objects we're going through in the loft began to expand exponentially. I would carry the bin bags back home, dump them in my room & then go out searching for more stuff. I surrounded myself with these objects in an attempt to insulate myself from a world that was turning cold. Hoarding Good Pop to ward off the Bad Pop.

I couldn't finish this contemplation of my collection without showing you this one. It's a carrier I got when I bought some toothpaste in a chemist's in Toronto, Canada, in autumn 2017. I was overjoyed.

The plastic this bag is made from is so gossamer-thin that I had to put a sheet of paper inside it when I took this photo, otherwise you wouldn't be able to read the message printed on it. The message reads: 'Your Life Store'.

That's what I thought at one time. That life is like an empty carrier bag that you choose to fill with whatever takes your fancy. And that if you overfill the bag then the handles will snap & won't that be a mess? That happened to me a number of times on the way home from jumble sales. Then I would throw the ruptured bag in a dark corner of the bedroom to be dealt with at a later date. Like now.

But look at this carrier: it's so flimsy that if you were to pick it up too quickly the handles would probably snap just from the weight of that one sheet of paper. Is that a metaphor? Could 'your life story' be that fragile?

Whatever. It's a keeper.

Chapter Twenty

I got ill a lot when I was living in the flat on the top floor of the old factory with my friend Tim.

As I mentioned, the flat had no heating – plus, the late nights at The Limit combined with a less than healthy diet didn't help. I can't say for sure that the Lemsip sachet overleaf dates from that period but it certainly reminds me of it. I haven't come across an online network of vintage over-the-counter medication collectors willing to pay big bucks for dead stock so I think we can safely put this in the 'COB' pile. (Wow – my head feels clearer already.)

My bedroom in the flat contributed to my near-constant state of illness. Tim had allocated me a tiny box room at the top of a flight of stairs. It was the highest room in the whole building. King of the castle – but very pokey. Then I spotted a small hatch in the wall. I removed it & – open sesame! – I was gazing into a massive loft space. It was directly under the roof so it tapered to a point in the middle & was divided into sections by massive metal girders. You could see chinks of light coming through the roof tiles in places – it was practically open to the elements. No matter – this was the room for me! I took a sledgehammer to the thin plasterboard wall & twenty minutes later I had my own downtown loft. Now where could I have got an idea like that from?

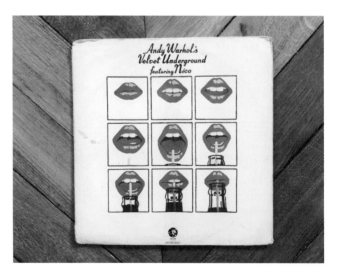

I've cheated a bit here because I would never lock this Velvet Underground album away in the dark with all this junk. That would be cruel. But it's an essential part of the story, so I just had to show it to you. (KEEP – for ever.)

I'd heard the name The Velvet Underground before but I only really took notice when Pulp got compared to them in another very early review in one of the photocopied Sheffield fanzines (*NMX*, I think). Perhaps it was our semi-acoustic instruments & tendency to be a little out of tune. Anyway, the comparison had been complimentary so that sent me off on a mission to actually hear them. That wasn't easy – like I said, albums 'disappeared' back in those days – & I scoured Sheffield's record shops in vain until I finally discovered this compilation in the local branch of HMV. It comprises all the tracks from their first album (except 'I'll Be Your Mirror'), four tracks from *White Light / White Heat* & three from the third, eponymous album. I've only learnt that information since – this was the format in which I first experienced The Velvet Underground – so the very first song of theirs I ever heard was 'I'm Waiting For My Man'. 'OK,' I thought, 'so they're a rock group.' That song was immediately followed by 'Candy Says', a beautiful, fragile number with 'Doo, doo, wah' backing vocals. 'OK – so they're a rock group & occasional melodic balladeers.' Side 1 finishes with 'All Tomorrow's Parties'. 'OK – hold on a minute now, because we've got a woman singing in a weird foreign accent over the top of some music that sounds almost modern classical.' My teenage brain was overloaded – they had been at least three different bands, all within the space of one side of an album. & this was expanded to four once the avant-garde noise of 'Sister Ray' kicked off Side 3.

Once again, we are discussing a band from the accepted canon of greats (there's a reason for that: they ARE great) so, once again, there is a lot of information about The Velvet Underground out there already. For me, the Velvets were very important because they created a bridge between The Beatles &

Punk. The Beatles were inspirational & opened the floodgates because they showed what kids from ordinary backgrounds COULD do – but there was no way I could ever seriously imagine myself being able to write songs with their exceptional level of musicality. After a few years in a band, I could still only master about four numbers from *The Beatles Complete Songbook*. The rest were beyond my reach (still are).

The Velvets came from the same era as The Beatles, & shared some of their gift for melody, but they also sometimes made a big noise like punk bands. & the production was rough around the edges – almost like you were listening to a rehearsal tape. It was certainly a lot easier to aspire to sounding like The Velvet Underground than to sounding like The Beatles – you just had to decide which Velvet Underground you wanted to be. Ever the over-reacher, I decided to have a go at all four.

Yet another dimension to the band came in the form of that hand-drawn logo above the image on the front cover, 'Andy Warhol's Velvet Underground featuring Nico'. This wasn't just a band: it had something to do with art, too.

Here was another similarity with The Beatles: the connection with contemporary artists. But it didn't say 'Peter Blake's Beatles' on the cover of *Sgt. Pepper* – how come this guy Andy Warhol got first mention on the front of this album? Not only on the front cover but in the sleeve notes too: 'The image of Andy Warhol is in fact mysterious. He is a cult hero, famous for his prints, for his painting & for his films . . . His desire to involve his audience in a total experience led him to open his own club, The Velvet Underground, in the centre of the hip community of New York.'

Andy Warhol sounded interesting – I decided to find out more about him. I went down to Sheffield Central Library & took out a book called *Popism – The Warhol Sixties* which turned out to be pretty much Warhol's diary from the decade in question. I've since discovered that it was transcribed from reels of audio tape made at the time. This gave the book a very accessible, gossipy feel – not at all like the highbrow 'art' treatise I was expecting. It was more the kind of stuff people would talk about down The Limit: who got off with who, how to lose weight, who got drunk at last week's party. One chapter was called 'Champagne Chins & Beer Bellies'.

The people featured in *Popism* lived in loft apartments & congregated around Warhol's studio, 'The Factory'. & that's the reason I sledgehammered myself a loft apartment & was living above a real factory in 'downtown' Sheffield. It was all The Velvet Underground's fault. The pop/art/music/party life described in *Popism* sounded like a lot of fun. Certainly more fun than Thatcherism.

I don't know whether I wrote 'LIFE IS ELSEWHERE' on the back of this envelope to remind myself to check out the Milan Kundera book of the same name or simply because the phrase appealed to me. It fell out of a pile of papers in another dark corner of our present loft. The fact that the entire back of the envelope has been dedicated to just these three words is significant: I must have thought this was an important phrase to remember. KEEP.

There's always a temptation to think that 'life is elsewhere'. To believe that you are somehow missing out on the real deal due to the area/historical epoch/social class you have been born into. 'I wish that I was born a thousand years ago,' wrote Lou Reed in 'Heroin' (Track 1, Side 2). Lou's imagined 'real deal' was sailing the 'darkened seas on a great big clipper ship'.

Now my fantasy 'elsewhere' was the New York of a mere twenty years ago: 'Let's bring '60s New York to '80s South Yorkshire,' I thought. How hard could that be? (Ironically enough, the same New York Lou Reed was wishing himself away from in the lyrics to 'Heroin'.)

Let me give you a more detailed picture of Life at The Factory (Sheffield Edition).

I had first met Tim Allcard about a year before the photos on the previous page were taken. I went to the Hallamshire Hotel one night & there was a band called In a Bell Jar on. They were unlike anything I'd ever seen before. First of all, they didn't have any 'normal' instruments – it was all percussion, a lot of it home-made. The most noticeable example of this was Tim's 'drum kit', which consisted of two large tin containers for cooking oil – the type you see discarded outside fast-food outlets. Tim had removed the top end from each & suspended them from a hand-built wooden frame. Impressive. He played the 'drums' using sticks with large balls of knotted rubber bands on the ends. The principle was similar to that of the pans used by a steel band (made from old oil drums) but the sound was much thinner & harsher (& louder).

There were various other hand drums & bells, & Tim & two other men took it in turns to chant or recite poetry. Ethereal female vocals could be heard from time to time. It wasn't until halfway through the concert that I realised they were coming from behind a sheet hung up in one corner of the stage. I was entranced. One song was about waiting for a bus. Another was about two lovers going swimming in a lake at night then getting tangled in some weeds & drowning. Although there was no conventional instrumentation, the music was very accessible. It seemed like I was witnessing the birth of a completely new musical genre. Here, in Sheffield – right on my doorstep.

Talking to Tim after the concert I asked him who the women singing behind the sheet were & he introduced me to them. One of them went on to become my first long-term girlfriend (yes, the same one who gave me that Marianne Faithfull album for Christmas). A pivotal evening.

A few months later, when I told Tim that my mother had been hinting I might want to consider leaving home now that I was out of school, he suggested I move into the new flat he had above a disused factory on Sheldon Row, just off The Wicker. (The Wicker being a wide straight road near the city centre with a brewery at one end & a large railway viaduct, known as The Wicker Arches, at the other.) Yes, please.

Our Factory was officially called 'Sheldon Row' but most people simply called the building complex we were living in 'The Wicker'. Since it had ceased to function as a factory it had been divided up into a number of 'mixed use' units. & there certainly was quite a 'mix' of uses: two garages, ten band rehearsal rooms, one model railway enthusiasts' club (very impressive track layout), one recording studio, one printer's, two table tennis clubs (a feud developed between them & they started shitting outside each other's doors – nasty), an accountant's & a karate dojo. & that's just off the top of my head – I'm sure there were more.

Tim's job was to act as caretaker for the whole building – his payment being that he was allowed to live in the flat on the top floor rent-free.

To move out of home straight into such an unconventional environment was a dream come true for me. A new chapter of life was beginning. & it was full of 'incident', as they say. Time for the Real Thing.

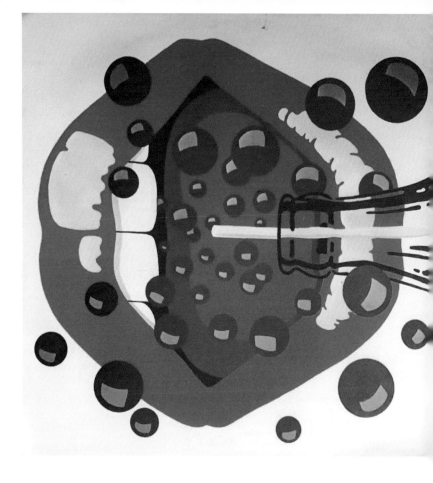

This is the image on the inside of the gatefold of my Velvet Underground album. I bet Andy Warhol was mad as hell when he saw this picture – someone at the record company has commissioned a kind of 'cover version' of one of his paintings. Big red lips sucking on a bottle of Coca-Cola. Fizzy Pop Art.

But he'd brought it on himself: Warhol's genius move was to get people to reappraise the contents of their rubbish bins. Until he came along a Campbell's soup can was just a container for soup. & a Coke bottle was just a Coke bottle. He changed the way people saw the everyday world around them. & once he'd

done that, the whole world jumped on the pop bandwagon. Including the guy in the record company art department.

The Pulp idea – the concept that you can find artistic depth & sustenance in the things other people throw away – wouldn't have been possible without my exposure to this record & ideas from the scene that gave birth to it. Pop was empowerment. It was accessible to everyone – all you needed to do was turn on the radio or TV or open a magazine. Pop was made to satisfy primal desires. Mass production let the genie out of the bottle – & it opened with a 'pop!'

Andy Warhol was maybe the first to hear that 'Pop'. To him it was the sound of a starting pistol. He quit his job as an advertising illustrator & rented a studio space. He started the '60s as a New York art world joke – & ended the decade as the most successful artist in the world.

The image in the centrefold of this Velvet Underground compilation may be a bad cover version of an Andy Warhol painting but this record is also the Real Thing. This is how I discovered the Velvets. & 'Andy Warhol's Velvet Underground featuring Nico' is the very best of Good Pop.

It's Pop to base your life around.

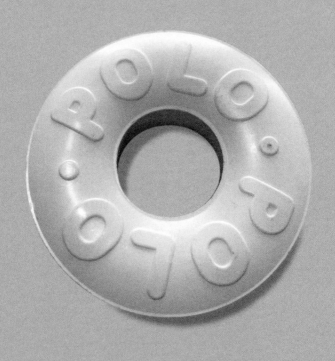

Chapter Twenty One

Let's freshen up.

This photo over the page isn't of a normal Polo mint. It's a white plastic dispenser in the shape of a Polo mint, about six centimetres in diameter. At one time it contained mini Polos. All gone now, I'm afraid. COB, you say? Well, hold on: this could be another one for the SELL ON EBAY pile – an unopened example, still containing its (well-past-their-sell-by-date) mints goes for £45 on today's market & an empty dispenser, such as we have here, will still set you back £20. We are sitting on a gold mine, my friend!

These dispensers were manufactured in the mid-1990s but I'm showing it to you now because Polos remind me of a particular story related to the time I was living at The Wicker in the mid-'80s.

As you can imagine, the fact that Tim & I had a penthouse apartment right in the centre of town at a time when most people we knew were on social security benefits led to us having a lot of visitors. Word spread. We were a popular stop-off point on the 'dole-strolling' scene in Sheffield. People would come round for a cup of tea & stay all day. That got wearing after a while. So Tim came up with an ingenious method to prevent people outstaying their welcome. He got rid of all the chairs.

It really worked. Once people realised there was nowhere to sit down & get comfortable they would finish their tea & then amble off to their next destination. Mission accomplished. It made mealtimes a little difficult though. No one likes to eat their dinner standing up. Very hard to cut up your food. Luckily, Tim had anticipated this problem. From somewhere he proudly produced two rectangular tin trays with fold-out wire legs attached to them. They were the kind of contraption you would use to serve a meal to a bed-ridden pensioner. My tray had a painting of a woodland scene printed on it. For the next three years every mealtime involved sitting on the kitchen floor, back propped against the wall, legs stretched out straight in front of me, eating off my 'granny tray'.

There were other rules of the house. No television. No meat. & no bass. Tim was of the opinion that music technology had peaked with the invention of the 78 rpm shellac disc & so music in the flat came via his collection of wind-up gramophones. He loved their abrasive, trebly sound – no bass frequencies whatsoever. To me they sounded unbearably tinny. Prolonged exposure made going to The Limit in the evening & standing near the bass bins in the sound system feel positively luxurious.

Though life at The Wicker was pretty spartan there was never any shortage of people asking if they could 'crash' there for a short while. Tim usually rebuffed these requests but he would occasionally make an exception. When one of his In a Bell Jar bandmates got his girlfriend pregnant, the couple & their newborn baby were allowed to set up home in the living room whilst looking for a flat of their own. The main memory I have of that time is when the baby (a boy) urinated near an electric fire & almost got electrocuted.

Another exception was a man called Dave. Dave had been a schoolmate of Tim's. At school he had been addicted to Polo mints – he would get through two tubes every day. As a consequence, by the time he left school aged sixteen, he had no teeth left. (This was in the days before sugar-free Polos were introduced on to the mint scene.) Now he had a set of false teeth & his addiction had switched to alcohol. Tim took pity on him because he had just been kicked out of the band he was in (the band went on to become ABC & had a number of international hit records – poor old Dave) & had been told by his parents he couldn't live at home any more due to his drinking.

Dave was allowed to stay at The Wicker on one condition: no drinking on the premises. I guess Tim was hoping that he would 'dry out' during his stay & thus be able to take better control of his life moving forward. Tough love.

Dave turned out to be a gentle, doe-eyed guy who spoke quietly, with a slight lisp due to his dentures. He was a good housemate. He behaved impeccably during the three months he stayed with us. No trouble whatsoever. & at the end of his stay he shook both our hands & thanked us profusely for all our help.

A week or so later the discoveries began.

Tim found the first one. He was clearing out a cupboard in the hall & found an empty quarter-bottle of Bell's whisky hidden at the back of it. That was enough to raise the alarm. We looked under the bed in the room Dave had stayed in. A stash of the same small, rectangular bottles. All empty. From that day on 'hunt the bottle' became a popular game whenever we got bored. Dave had been inventive in choosing his hiding places. Chances were if you had to move an item of furniture or do some work in a dark, forgotten corner of the flat you would end up coming across a couple of bottles stashed away. We lost count of the number we found. &, just when we thought there couldn't possibly be any more left to find, a new, rich source would open up. For instance, a year after Dave left we had a plumbing problem that led to the discovery of a dozen bottles in the cold-water cistern in the bathroom. Crafty old Dave.

The weird thing was that neither of us had suspected anything whilst Dave was living with us. He had been affable & polite & never acted like he was inebriated. We certainly never smelt alcohol on his breath. I guess his old Polo habit must have come in useful there. He could devour as many tubes a day as he wanted now that he was wearing false teeth. Clever old Dave.

I relate the Story of Dave to try & give something of the atmosphere of Sheffield in the mid-'80s. The recession was starting to bite & there were a lot of lost souls on the street.

Regular visitors to The Wicker included Crazy John (the name says it all), Rabid (an aggressive punk from Chesterfield who transformed into a pleasant & placid guy after sniffing glue & drinking undiluted orange squash), Deano (a heroin addict with a pet rat that would shit in all four corners of the kitchen, then pile the droppings together in just one corner & start all over again) & General Dyson (a Bowie lookalike who had suffered a mental breakdown after being attacked by some

skinheads whilst he was on an acid trip – he now wore military fatigues & sported a child's toy rifle slung over his shoulder).

There were many, many others. Some days we disconnected the doorbell. & I couldn't pretend that I was immune to the general malaise: my jumble sale habit was out of control. My bedroom was full of black bin liners – many of them unopened since I'd brought them into the flat. I just couldn't stop. What had started as a way of insulating myself against the harshness of the present moment was now threatening to smother me.

So what prevented me from joining the legion of lost souls? Why, the band.

The photos on the previous page are from a session taken by local photographer David 'Bod' Bocking down at The Wicker in June 1985. They provide a perfect opportunity to get to know a new iteration of the band – especially because one or two of the members survived into the line-up· of Pulp that eventually

achieved some success a decade later. Who should I introduce you to first?

I think it's going to have to be Russell.

I love these little photo strips that Bod printed of the band members. It's like he was thinking of making a Pulp photo-dominoes set – or maybe one of those memory-based card games? Russell Senior is the right way up in the picture to the left. You've actually met him already (sort of): he was the person who wrote that first live review of Pulp at the Leadmill festival in his fanzine *The Bath Banker*, the one that ended with the lines, 'VAST CHEERING FOR ENCORE'.

Russell came down to the fish market where I had my Saturday job a couple of weeks after the concert & sold me a copy of the fanzine. I was impressed because it came with a free fortune-telling fish. I think I still have it somewhere . . .

Are you familiar with the 'Fortune Teller Miracle Fish'? It's made out of very thin cellophane & you place it on the palm of your hand & then observe how it behaves. A moving head indicates 'jealousy' whereas a moving tail denotes 'indifference'. (I'm reading this off the back of the tiny envelope the fish is housed in.) Moving head & tail tells you that you're 'in love' & if the fish remains motionless that means you are a 'dead one'. A very 'Pulp' item. A love oracle made out of the same material as that gossamer-thin carrier bag I showed you earlier. KEEP.

Russell also invited me to a party the following week at his dad's house in Gleadless – which gave me the chance to find out more about him. He was a couple of years older than me & was studying politics at Bath University (hence the name of his fanzine). He came back to Sheffield one or two weekends a month to see his girlfriend Sandra. He was into cooking – at one point in the party he made everyone taste a '100-year-old egg' that he'd prepared himself. It was foul. He had a friend called 'Quasi' (due to his supposed resemblance to the Hunchback of Notre Dame as played by Charles Laughton). He was an expert on wild mushrooms & often went out foraging in the woods. & he was into unusual bands I'd never heard of. Around 2 a.m. he put on *D.o.A: the Third & Final Report of Throbbing Gristle*. I remember hearing the song 'Hamburger Lady' & reading the album sleeve notes that explained what the song was about & getting completely freaked out. I left soon after that & I recall looking at all the houses I passed on the walk home & wondering what strange mysteries they might contain.

Russell seemed grown up but in an encouraging way. He was sophisticated & intriguing & surprising. Meeting him was certainly a stroke of good fortune for me.

He was also the reason that the band still existed at this moment in time. Russell returned to Sheffield when his university course ended & asked what I was up to musically. At that point I was ready to go & take up the place I'd been deferring to read English at Liverpool University. I was disillusioned by my lack of success since leaving school. The final straw had been when a member of the group jumped ship & joined The Mission. The Mission! I was now officially creatively inferior to a goth band – definitely time to jack it in.

Russell persuaded me to have one rehearsal with him to see if he could make me change my mind. We convened in the garage outside my mum's house, which had been the Pulp rehearsal facility ever since our John Peel session. My grandad had done another piece of creative wiring – this time running a 13-amp power supply in from the house via a hole in the wall. The plug for the power cable went into a socket next to the telephone in the hall &, when I dutifully unplugged it after every rehearsal (as I had been told I must), I needed to pull my jumper down over my hand in order to do so because otherwise the plug was too hot to handle. Health & safety nightmare.

Russell also invited Magnus Doyle (you'll meet him soon) to the rehearsal. Magnus had been playing percussion in recent line-ups of Pulp. Russell immediately set the agenda for the rehearsal by teaching us one of HIS songs. He'd been in a group called The Masons at university & had a song called 'Maureen' dating from this time. The song was in a dark rockabilly style. A fast, choppy guitar riff with barely intelligible, barked vocals over the top. From what I could make out, 'Maureen' seemed to be a woman in a red dress who liked running over people in her red car. Russell informed me that the song's male protagonist was sexually excited by this behaviour. He suggested that I finish the lyrics off for him, with a view to singing it myself. 'Think J. G. Ballard's *Crash* transposed to the Redcar Races,' he said helpfully. It felt like getting homework again. Except that I liked it.

I had got used to being the only one in the group who instigated ideas for songs. Now, I was jolted out of my complacency. This was exciting. This music was abrasive & awkward – but it was also alive. & it was *about* something. Even if that something happened to be an extreme form of auto-erotica. It wasn't just music for music's sake – a pretty noise. There was a story & an attitude. & it was fun. Within half an hour I knew I was never going to study English at university.

Another of Bod's photo-dominoes. As promised, here's Magnus Doyle: 'Mag' was an exceptional & very unusual drummer. In fact, he was (& still is) an exceptional & very unusual person. You could tell that from your very first encounter with him – even from a distance. His hair was a big clue. You can't see it so well in this photo because it's taken against a dark background but Mag's hair was always ... striking. At this moment in time it was cut in a style that, in silhouette, made it look like he was sporting a matador's hat. Prior to that he had shaved the top of his head & left the rest of his hair long to replicate the look of a Cistercian monk. It was

interesting to see what new style Mag would be trying out when our rehearsal time came around.

After we'd decided to persevere with the group, Mag suggested that his friend Peter 'Manners' Mansell join as bass player.

Manners was considerably younger than the rest of us – seventeen when he joined the band. No matter: the important thing was that he was available & he owned a bass guitar. Looking back, it seems unusual that he was friends with Mag because, compared to Mag's very individual sense of style, he was pretty straight. He wore skinhead clothes like Harrington jackets & Doc Martens boots. He worked part-time as a postman & had stopped going to school when he was fourteen. Pete was very enthusiastic about joining the band & was all for the new, more aggressive sound. He was the young gun of the group.

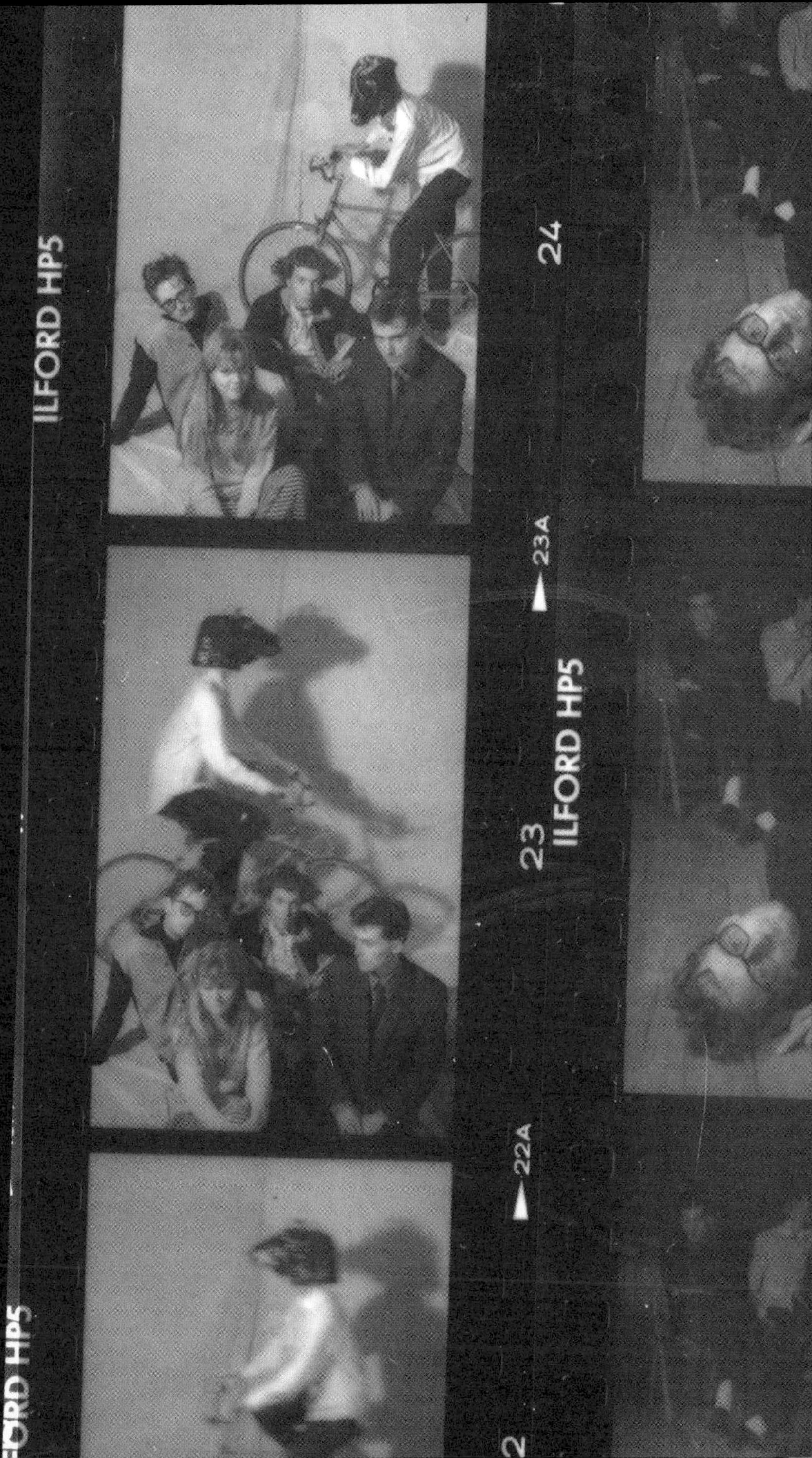
ILFORD HP5
24
23A
23
ILFORD HP5
22A

You can get some of that sense of fun from another shot on the contact sheet (see previous page). The shoot took place in the large unit directly below the flat I shared with Tim (scene of one of the infamous table tennis club 'dirty protests' I told you about earlier) now enjoying a brief tenure as home to a street theatre troupe called 'Tingel Tangle'.

There were one or two props lying around the place & Manners spotted a papier mâché dog's head & decided to wear it. I was familiar with this dog's head. I'd attended a rehearsal by the theatre troupe a week or so before & seen it used in a 'sketch' protesting against the use of animals in medical experiments. Hearing a self-trained actor, wearing a papier mâché dog's head, declaim the words, 'How can they be so kind & then so cruel?' over & over again in a pained, high-pitched (yet muffled) voice is the moment that put me off street theatre for life.

For Manners this canine headpiece wasn't enough on its own so he decided to ride a bike through shot whilst wearing it. I don't know if you can tell but the rest of us are all trying very hard not to laugh on camera. You can see that we're a disparate bunch: Mag's matador hairstyle is more apparent in this picture, Russell looks like he just came from the office, I appear to be wearing a Captain Scarlet tunic – & who's that sitting in the foreground?

Candida Mary Doyle is the other member of this line-up who endured through to the days when Pulp found success in the mid-1990s. She is Magnus's older sister & at the time was going out with Manners. She became our keyboard player.

After the John Peel session in 1981 the group bought some new equipment with the money we were paid by the BBC. The largest of these items was a Farfisa electric organ that I had spotted in a junk shop opposite Sheffield cathedral.

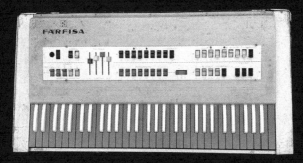

The reason I bought it was the colour scheme. As you can see, it has grey keys where the white ones would normally be & white ones in place of the black keys. I thought that must mean it was capable of playing different notes to those obtainable by conventional instruments & would help us access new musical realms. (I've since seen photos of the same model of organ being used by Can, Sly & the Family Stone, & Sun Ra, so maybe that isn't such a preposterous idea after all.) Candida certainly took us into a new realm. Not just musically (although, with her Grade 3 in piano, she was by far & away the most technically qualified member of the band) but due to the simple fact that she was a woman.

Being in a band is often a blokey, macho environment & the fact that Candida was around stopped that happening to us. She was an integral part of our music & that gave the band a whole new dynamic. She was one of the gang – so the gang had to adapt to her. I'm not saying the rest of us all became 'new men' overnight but it's no coincidence that it wasn't until Candida joined that the second 'classic' line-up of Pulp was complete. Candida's influence can't really be overstated.

The first concert we played with this new line-up was a real hoot.

It took place at Brunel University on 7 February 1984. We'd been booked by a friend of Russell's who then cancelled the show. We decided to pretend we hadn't received this information & turn up to play anyway. We were that keen to lay our new sound on a live audience. What we didn't know was that, in the interim, the Ents Committee had booked a rugby songs band called Ivor Biggun & the Hefty Cocks to play instead of us. Weirdly enough, they ended up cancelling at the last minute but the upshot was that our audience on the night basically comprised of the university rugby club. Not our target demographic – & definitely not 'new men'. Our soundcheck had been interrupted by some of them coming into the hall & playing 'dirty biscuit'. (I'll let you google that term to discover just how disgusting a practice it is.)

We started the concert by plugging in an old air-raid siren that Tim had found in the roof space of The Wicker & sounding the alarm for five minutes. That certainly got the crowd's attention – it was incredibly loud in a confined space. Those five minutes seemed to last for ever. Then we launched into 'Maureen'. That went down OK – or maybe the crowd were still shell-shocked from the noise of the siren. Things started to degenerate when Tim joined us on stage to read some of his poetry. It was becoming apparent to the audience that this was not going to be a night of ribald 'rugger' singalongs. The heckling & booing began in earnest. We launched into another song but, about a minute in, a guy came to the front of the stage, pulled his trousers down and mooned us. I, quite naturally under the circumstances, kicked his bare backside. A self-appointed master of ceremonies suddenly appeared on stage, seized the mic & bellowed, 'Gentlemen, I'd like you to thank Pulp,' indicating that, as far as he was concerned, the concert was over. I wrestled him to the ground in protest & a stage invasion ensued. I managed to squeeze out from under his bulk in the melee & made a run for the dressing room. The rest of the band were already there. We slid the fridge containing our rider in front of the door to prevent the angry mob following me in. There was frantic hammering & kicking & Russell & Mag had to sit on the fridge to keep the rugger louts from breaching our defences & exacting revenge. We were all grinning deliriously – it was a proper riot! Manners was particularly excited. He was bouncing around the room shouting, 'Rebels of '84!' What a perfect start to the new era.

Here are the Rebels of '84 just over a year later. The reason we gathered together in the old table tennis club was that we needed a photo to go on the cover of the first record release by this new version of Pulp. I don't think this picture was ever a serious contender, though looking back it would have been quite appropriate. We're all staring off in completely different directions. Perhaps Bod's instruction to us had been, 'Look wherever you want – just as long as it's *not* at the camera!'

The photo sums us up as a band at that time – we were all wildly contrasting characters. It was so different to being in a band with people you'd gone to school with, where you all had a shared background & frame of reference. The only thing the current line-up of Pulp had in common was the fact we were in a group with each other. That was it. & that made it more

exciting. We were together because we had a cause! Something bigger than any of us as individuals. That made the band a real life-saver.

Take Two: In this next photo three fifths of the band *are* making eye contact with the viewer – but this is undercut by the fact that Peter 'Manners' Mansell is hiding. Can you spot him? His backlit, shadowy presence is visible just by Candida's left shoulder. We were making use of one of the theatre group's sets & Manners thought he was adding some intrigue to the image by concealing himself. Maybe

I thought I was adding a touch of sophistication by sitting on a high stool. Smooth.

Take Three: bingo! I spotted that the door to the bathroom in the unit had a pane of textured glass in it. Designed to give occupants a little privacy & all that. But if you put your eyes right up to this window you saw the scene beyond split into horizontal, diffracted bands. I thought it was a great effect & showed it to Bod. He immediately set about installing his tripod & camera behind the closed door in 'the facilities'. I admired his dedication to his craft. He said the resulting image would be too 'vague' if we all stayed at a distance & so asked for a volunteer to come right up to the glass & peer through it at him. As the lead track on the record we were releasing was called 'Little Girl (With Blue Eyes)' it seemed logical to suggest that Candida take centre-stage. She stepped up & – hey presto! – we had our cover image.

(Examining the picture closely it would appear that Manners is still sporting the papier mâché dog's head we saw him in earlier.)

PULP

LITTLE GIRL
(WITH.BLUE.EYES)

AND OTHER PIECES...

FIRE 5

Jarvis Cocker

Russell Senior

Candida Doyle

Manners

Magnus Doyle

Side 1 LITTLE GIRL
(WITH.BLUE.EYES)

Side 2 SIMULTANEOUS
BLUE GLOW
THE WILL TO POWER

ALL THE SONGS WRITTEN BY
PULP
and Published by
TWIST and SHOUT MUSIC
RECORDED IN JUNE 1985 by
SIMON HINKLER
SLEEVE DESIGNED BY PULP
and JULIE PARAMORE.
PHOTOGRAPHS TAKEN.BY.
DAVID BOCKING (0742) 681362.
THANKS: TIM. JOHN.TONI.CLIVE

Fire records 12 Kingdon Road London NW8 1PH Tel 794 7304

"Distribution by Nine Mile and the Cartel"

of the 'toilet door' picture in the end). The hand lettering was done by Julie Paramore – one of the mysterious women singing from behind the sheet at that In a Bell Jar concert I went to. She was the first person to show me the work of Egon Schiele & Gustav Klimt & this calligraphy is heavily influenced by the style of the Vienna Secession movement that both those artists are associated with. Another Art Scene to draw inspiration from.

Speaking of which, the record inside the sleeve had four tracks on it – & at least three of them had the fingerprints of The Velvet Underground all over them.

'Little Girl (With Blue Eyes)' – the 'lead' track – mines the influence of the Melodic Velvets songs such as 'New Age' & 'Pale Blue Eyes'. Turn the record over & 'Simultaneous' is a pretty good stab at recreating the sound of John Cale-era Velvets. Russell had been inspired by the Welshman's example & so taught himself to play the violin. You can hear echoes of 'Heroin' & 'Venus in Furs' in his parts. The final track on the EP is 'Will to Power' – a song written & sung by Russell – which owes more to the Noisy Velvets of 'Sister Ray' & 'European Son'. There's no bass on this song so Manners just screamed in the background during the loud parts.

You can try your darnedest to replicate something but you'll never get it exactly right. & the ways in which it's 'wrong' – i.e. the ways in which it differs from the original – that's YOU. For better or for worse.

Here's an example of 'for the worse'. These 'Top of the Pops' records used to be everywhere. Not just in record shops. They sold them in the sweet shop in front of my mum's house in Intake. The first in the series was released in 1968 & the formula remained the same until they were discontinued in 1985: hits of the day 'recreated' by an anonymous studio band (sometimes credited as the 'Top of the Poppers'), attractive woman on the front cover, rock-bottom price. This particular record has a certain notoriety because the Top of the Poppers have a stab at 'Death Disco' by Public Image Ltd & the result is quite something to experience. (But only once in a single human lifetime.)

Usually I avoided these records like the plague when I came across them at jumble sales but this one I had to hear. The Top of the Poppers' attempt at being PiL fails because, at heart, they're just a bunch of session musicians playing to pay the rent. They don't care about the song or the band. & you can hear that in their performance. The disconnect is very comical. The original idea behind these albums must have been, 'It's all worthless trash anyway so the kids won't be able to tell the difference.' But of course we could. Telling the difference was a matter of life & death. We cared a lot about the Pop we fell in love with. & this record is extremely Bad Pop. COB.

The Velvet Underground, as previously noted, are extremely Good Pop. The only band all five members of Pulp could agree were 'Major'. We had nothing to gain financially by attempting to sound like them (unlike the Top of the Poppers). For us they were more a signpost to follow – a beacon to steer by.

Was getting Candida in the band inspired by the example of Moe Tucker, female drummer in the Velvets? Well, in as much as it proved that a woman could be an equal member of a band rather than merely a decorative addition to one, yes. The very best bands do this: they inspire by example. They say, 'Go ahead: it's OK to do your own thing – that's all we ever did.'

By aiming at being the Velvet Underground we ended up discovering ourselves.

At least this photo of Russell & myself didn't end up on the cover of the 'Little Girl' record. I'd like to point out that this 'topless' pose was Russell's idea. Was it his attempt at a 'cheesecake' image such as those used on the 'Top of the Pops' albums? Or was it more an homage to D.A.F., one of his favourite bands at the time? Whatever the inspiration, it quite rightly ended up on the 'reject' pile. Glad I found it up here though. (& glad I kept my vest on.)

By the last months of 1985 we had a new band, a new sensibility, a new image & a new record about to be released. We had come a long way. Pulp #2 was ready to go.

& then I went & spoilt it all by falling out of a window.

Chapter Twenty-Two

One of my favoured ways of dealing with the horror of Thatcher's Britain was to sleep a lot.

Plus, sleeping was cheap – useful when you're subsisting on £30 a week.

Sleeping a lot is a habit that's stuck even though the Iron Lady is long gone. When I was on *Desert Island Discs* in 2005 I chose a bed as my luxury item. You can deal with anything if you've had a good night's sleep.

The photo at the head of this chapter is of my alarm clock from The Wicker days. Each morning I was awoken by a Dancing Lady (rather than an Iron one). The clock is made from cream plastic &, next to the clockface, has a compartment with a glass front containing a tiny model of a ballerina. When the alarm goes off, instead of being jolted from your dreams by the unpleasant ringing of a bell you are gently coaxed out of oblivion by the melodious chimes of a music box.* Whilst the music is playing the ballerina performs pirouettes within her tiny mirrored cell. Her legs are jointed beneath the tutu she's wearing so her movements are weirdly lifelike.

Now, doesn't that sound like a charming & inspiring way to start the day? Dancing your way into consciousness. Well, in reality it was depressing as hell because as the mechanism of the alarm wound down, the music became slower & slower & the ballerina's movements more disjointed and jerky. Imagine being woken every morning to witness the climactic scenes of Powell & Pressburger's *The Red Shoes*. (Great film: Moira Shearer dons a pair of magic ballet shoes & literally dances herself to death.) A 'weepie' first thing every morning was a bit much. It cast a long shadow over the rest of the day. Eventually I got tired of 'intimations of mortality' every time I woke up & bought a cheap radio alarm.

What to do with this clock now? I'm sorry, Tiny Dancer, but your prima ballerina days are over – time to perform your final *pas de deux* en route to the COB pile over there.

---

* I don't know what the piece of music is called but I've heard a 'humorous' song sung to the same tune: 'Do you recall on the night we first met? / We danced until dawn for the room had no bed.' Ring any bells?

Cocker comes a cropper

Jarvis Cocker — recovering.

SHEFFIELD band Pulp have had to cancel concerts for the next few weeks — because singer Jarvis Cocker has fallen out of a window.

Cocker, who is now in the Royal Hallamshire Hospital, suffered a number of broken bones in his leg, hip, arm and wrist, when he fell 20 foot to the pavement.

The blow has come at a crucial time for the band who have just released their Little Girl (With Blue Eyes) single and were due to play an important date at the Greyhound in London on December 11. Unless Cocker undergoes a miracle recovery this date looks almost certain to be cancelled.

They have also ran into problems with radio play for the single — one Radio Hallam deejay faded it out when he heard the chorus, and that was at one a.m.

*Winners of copies of Pulp's new single are E Wilson of Firshill Walk, Sheffield 4; and C Norton, of Toftwood Road, Crookes. Because of Cocker's mishap, the Greyhound tickets have now had to be withdrawn. The answer to Jarvis's question — "When was the Hole In The Road officially opened?" is November, 1967

Try as I might, I couldn't sleep my life away. I was due a wake-up call. A wake-up fall, actually.

Now: I have related the story of the accident described in this newspaper article many times over the years but it is such a 'road to Damascus' moment in my life story that I have to tell it again here. It had a profound effect on the direction my creativity took from then on. So don't fall asleep on me . . .

Here's how it was reported in the local newspaper: 'Sheffield band Pulp have had to cancel concerts for the next few weeks – because singer Jarvis Cocker has fallen out of a window.'

Factually correct – but a little . . . lacking in detail? Allow me to paint a more nuanced picture:

One night in early November 1985 I went to a girl's flat in the centre of Sheffield & tried to impress her by going out on to her window ledge & then re-entering her living room via the next window along. This idea had been put in my head by an incident at a party that had taken place at The Wicker the week before. A guest had performed the same trick in our kitchen & I was very taken with it. He slid up the sash window, stood on the window ledge & reached around the outside of the building to the adjacent window ledge about three feet away. He got a round of applause when he re-entered the room after his brief moment in the open air. Tim wasn't too happy though because the windows in question were a good fifty feet above the pavement & if the stunt had gone wrong the resulting fall would have been deadly. That would have brought our tenancy to an abrupt end. Not a good thing to have on a caretaker's CV.

My attempt to emulate the trick seven days later was doomed to failure from the off. The window frames were all wrong for a start: they were modern metal frames with a hinge halfway up them. This meant that you opened the window by rotating the pane of glass within the window frame. The portion of window below the hinge protruded outside the building whilst the portion above intruded within the room. Keep pushing & the pane of glass will eventually end up horizontal within its frame. Maximum ventilation. Good news if you were finding the room stuffy but absolutely terrible news for me & what I had in mind. The guy at the Wicker party had been able to stand upright on our window ledge & simply 'walk' around the outside of the building. That was impossible with this type of window. So I came up with my own idea.

A terrible idea.

I decided I should crawl out of the window, hang by my fingers from the ledge & then swing over to the next window ledge before hoisting myself back into the room. Easy.

I've often been asked since whether I was drunk or high when I came up with this plan. The answer is neither. The girl in question & myself had simply encountered one of those pockets of awkwardness that can occur when you're alone with someone in an unfamiliar room & you're not sure what might happen next. I was just trying to lighten the atmosphere a bit, maybe impress her a little into the bargain. To her credit, the girl begged me not to go through with my plan. But to no avail.

Five minutes later I am hanging from the ledge, realising that I have seriously over-estimated my physical capabilities.

Just hanging there is taking pretty much all my strength. This marks the beginning of My Revelation – the foremost thought in my mind is how 'undramatic' this situation feels. If it was a scene in a film or a TV programme there would be tense orchestral music to heighten the atmosphere of peril. It feels too 'normal'. The dialogue isn't up to scratch either – I'm still trying to be polite & jokey: 'Hmmm – maybe this wasn't such a good idea after all. I think I'd better come back in.'

My Revelation deepens – I don't have the strength to get myself back in the room. I can't even pull my chin up as far as the ledge & I can tell I'm in danger of losing my grip. In our hypothetical film this would be the moment I'd find that extra ounce of strength & heroically drag myself back from the brink. But no sudden boost of energy is forthcoming. Somebody fire the scriptwriter!

I ask, in my calmest voice, whether there might be anyone else in the flat who could help pull me out of this predicament. The answer is negative.

We agree that it's not worth her attempting to rescue me on her own. I look down. Am I that high up? A double-decker bus drives by, bang on cue (they got that bit right). I can see the top of its roof so, yes, I am pretty high up. What next?

I tell her I'm going to attempt a 'controlled drop'. She's not keen on the idea. What do I even mean by that anyway? Falling is falling – how can there be anything 'controlled' about it? It's gravity. My logic is that it's better to let go consciously, & then fall straight down to hit the ground feet first, than it is to suddenly lose my grip, fall awkwardly & risk landing on my back. Or my head. She's still not keen. I tell her I'm going to count to three & then let go. She's just shaking her head & saying 'no' over & over again. She's still doing this as I begin to count.

1, 2, 3 . . .

Ouch.

to Jarvis
get
well
soon.

Here's a get-well card drawn by my cousin Emily in the aftermath of the 'controlled drop'. It appears that the nurse attending to me has fainted due to the extent of my injuries. Once again, the report of the incident in the *Star* is a little more deadpan: 'Cocker, who is now in the Royal Hallamshire Hospital, suffered a number of broken bones in his leg, hip, arm & wrist when he fell twenty foot to the pavement.' Back to the report from our man on the ground:

I know I'm in trouble before I even hit the pavement – because it's taking so long *to* hit the pavement. I seem to be sliding down that exterior wall for ever – but when I do make landfall I certainly know about it: the pain is unbelievable. How to describe it? Well, you know when you're walking around in your bare feet & you accidentally bang your little toe really hard against the bed base or a chair leg & the pain wells up to a crescendo & you hop around swearing until it slowly begins to subside? This is a bit like that except on a much bigger scale – & the pain never reaches the peak of the crescendo stage. It continues to rise & rise in intensity. Your brain cannot comprehend what is happening because the pain has exceeded the sensory capacities of the instrumentation designed to measure it. It's off the scale, as they say. & still it keeps growing – each second setting a new world record for 'amount of pain suffered during his lifetime by the human being known as Jarvis Branson Cocker'. (I'm glad to say that's a record that still stands.)

This constant medal-presentation ceremony going on in my mind renders any other mental processes difficult. Memories become patchy from this point on. I remember trying to stand up – PAIN! – I remember my right leg moving in an unnatural *sideways* manner – PAIN! – I remember sitting back down on the pavement (good move: my pelvis is fractured &, if I had put any more weight on it, it would have snapped in two) – PAIN! – I remember looking up & seeing the silhouette of a person in the open window I have just fallen from & calling up towards it, 'Do you think you could call an ambulance please?' – PAIN! – & then I remember being in an ambulance & it being very brightly lit – PAIN! – & then I am in a bed & it's dark – LESS PAIN (thank you, morphine) – & then I am still in bed but now it's light – STIIILLL LESSSS PAINNN! – & then I wake up & it's two days later & my mother & sister are sitting by the bed & I'm surrounded by cards like the one I showed you that my cousin Emily made me. Phew . . .

HANG IN THERE JARVIS love Adrienne xx xx

There's also this message from the girl I'd been attempting to show off in front of. She always did have a dry sense of humour.

My injuries are all on the right-hand side of my body. I have fractured my right wrist, the right-hand side of my pelvis & my right foot. The foot took the brunt of the fall & is pretty badly damaged. My pelvis is fractured but will heal given bed-rest. If it had completely snapped it would have been doubtful that I would ever walk again. The wrist is just a hairline fracture. I will be kept in the Hallamshire Hospital for a fortnight, after which I will be moved to the King Edward VII convalescent facility for at least a month.

Visitors & doctors are in general agreement that I am lucky. Lucky not to have landed on a parking meter. Lucky that the ambulance came quickly. Lucky that no passers-by attempted to move me. All this is true – but they still don't know the half of it. I'm the luckiest man alive.

My fall from grace has shaken something loose. I have fallen to earth with a bump. But in a good way. & I guess that's why I've mentioned this incident so many times in the past. Because I credit this as the moment my world view changed profoundly. Life is elsewhere? No: life is occurring, in all its intensity, right now – & right under your nose.

The scales had fallen from my eyes. (Must have been the impact when I hit the ground.) I now realised that I'd been surrounded by inspiration all along. Only I'd been too intent on scanning the distant horizon to actually see it. Now that I was back down at ground level & staring life fully in the face I found myself eyeball to eyeball with what I'd always been searching for: something to write about.

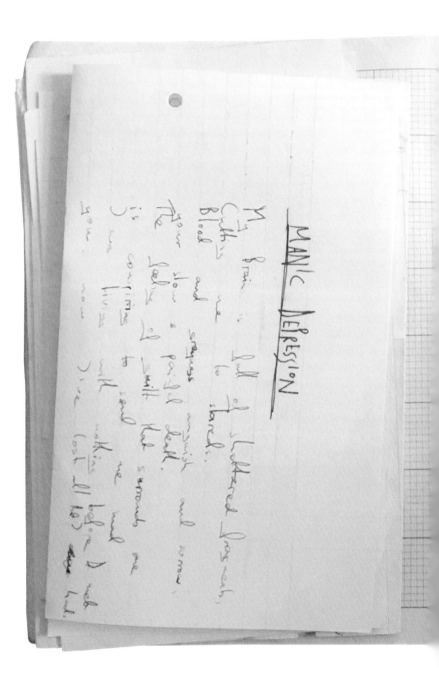

I SCRUBBED THE CRABS THAT KILLED SHEFFIELD

I arrived early on a Saturday
morning,
Some time after 8 o'clock.
I received no prior warning,
It all came on as a bit of a shock...
There were crabs all around me,
hundreds, thousands, quite a lot.
They'd been put in water, left
all overnight through the night, and now that they'd
died they had started to rot.

CHORUS

Oh-Woh Oh Oh - Oh Oh Oh Oh!!
I scrubbed, I scrubbed them,
Oh - Woh Oh - Oh Oh Oh Oh!!
I scrubbed the crabs that killed Sheffield

The stench was really quite amazing,
Still, we had a job to do.
In a while I heard some people
complaining,
But the terrible smell just grew &
grew.

315

My Revelation hadn't just come out of nowhere. There had been glimpses of it in the past. Examples of me using incidents from real life as creative inspiration.

Let's take a final look at the trusty 'Pulp Master Plan' exercise book.

We've already dealt with my very first lyric – the schoolboy humour of 'Shakespeare Rock' – but here we encounter the other side of the coin: teen angst. My equivalent of the sixth-form poetry that everyone is so embarrassed to re-read as an adult. It's a necessary rite of passage but it still makes me shudder.

There's a prime example in the preceding photo spread. On the left-hand page are lyrics to a song called 'Manic Depression'. A big subject. & just in case you were in any doubt as to just how big a subject it is I have helpfully written the title in RED INK (whereas the rest of the text is in green) – this is SERIOUS, OK? Pay attention. Now, what did I know about manic depression at the age of sixteen? Absolutely nothing. Nothing, that is, apart from the fact that it was a Major Issue – & songs are supposed to deal with weighty subjects like that, right?

Another early song called 'Life is a Circle' started with the words:

> *Life is a circle you're caught on*
> *Life is a road that's much too long*
> *It winds, goes ahead*
> *Only stops when you're dead*

Heavy.

My early songwriting oscillated wildly between the twin poles of immature jokiness & excruciating attempts at profundity. No, you can't have a look at any more. I'm sorely tempted to COB the lot – but I will allow you a brief glance at the song on the right side of the spread. A song rejoicing under the title of 'I Scrubbed the Crabs that Killed Sheffield'.

This title would seem to put it firmly in the 'jokiness' camp – but there's more here than first meets the eye. Yes: because this is the first-ever example of me trying to write about an event from my own life.

I've mentioned my Saturday job on a fishmonger's stall in Sheffield's Castle Market. The job had come through a scrap-metal merchant called John Hepplestone who my mum dated for a while. He thought I needed 'toughening up' & used his contacts down the market to secure me the position. The 'old boy network', South Yorkshire style.

The stall was called 'Grayson & Boaler' & was run by a man called Ron. The stall opposite ours sold tripe. That was an eye-opener. I was dimly aware of what tripe was but I'd never seen it in the . . . flesh. There was this stuff called 'honeycomb tripe' that came in big sheets that looked just like carpet underlay. It was stored in black plastic bins in front of the stall. Then there was the famous intestinal double act of 'Chitterling & Bag' festooned on hooks under the awning of the stall. Glistening under the strip lights like Christmas decorations direct from the abattoir. On my first day in the job I overheard an old lady saying to her companion, 'I don't mind chitterling but I'm not that keen on bag.' I could tell I was going to learn a lot from this place. Working across the aisle from the tripe stall was like working opposite a particularly gruesome Halloween *tableau vivant* – except that it ran all year long.

Our stall was rather tame in comparison. We specialised in crabs. Sheffield is 60 miles from the nearest coastline so that was quite a draw, actually. The crabs arrived from Grimsby & Hull packed in ice in wooden crates. The ice was meant to keep them alive during transit. My job was to transfer the crabs from the crates into a large metal sink, cover them in cold water, scrub them with a wire-bristle brush to remove mud & dirt & then put them in a large metal tub full of boiling water. That is also quite gruesome, now I come to think about it. But I quickly became immune to that aspect of the job. (I was just following orders, as they say.)

My main motivating factor was to get the crabs all scrubbed & boiled as quickly as possible without losing a finger to one of their powerful claws. I didn't want my musical career to be cut short by a seafood incident. Plus, once I'd completed my scrubbing chores I was free to do 'softer' work such as weighing out prawns or staring at that girl who worked on the petfood stall over the way.

The inspiration for 'I Scrubbed the Crabs that Killed Sheffield' came after I'd been in the job for a couple of months. I arrived at the market one Saturday morning to be greeted by an awful smell. Markets selling fresh meat and fish are of course full of pungent aromas but this was something of a different magnitude. As I walked through the market towards our stall the smell got stronger. & stronger. I soon found out why. Our stall was surrounded by piles of dead crabs.

The delivery of crabs had arrived on Friday evening rather than early Saturday morning as was usually the case. Ron had been called out of the pub to deal with this irregularity &, perhaps because he wasn't entirely sober, had elected to put the crabs in bins full of water to keep them alive. Bins full of tap water that is. Being accustomed to living in seawater the crabs, quite understandably under the circumstances, perished overnight & were now rotting en masse in front of Grayson & Boaler. Hence the incredibly unpleasant stench.

Ron was unrepentant. He immediately set me to work scrubbing the crabs & getting ready our first boiling of the day. The smell made me gag. The owners of surrounding stalls were complaining that the stink was keeping customers from coming into our part of the market. But Ron held firm. A first boiling was carried out. A few brave customers formed a queue. It was tradition on the stall that the fishmonger would open the crab to show the meat inside before a sale was made. I had been shown how to do this on my first day – you hold the crab in your left hand with its undercarriage exposed, hook the thumb of your right hand behind the crab's back legs, place the rest of your right hand flat against the crab's belly & then slowly prise the creature apart. All being well you will end up with the crab shell in your left hand & its legs & claws in the other. (Reverse instructions if you are left-handed.) You can then show the customer the meat in the shell cavity & also remove the poisonous gills (sometimes referred to as 'ladies' fingers') that surround the crab's mouthparts. Every crab taken from this first boiling discharged a disgusting brown slurry when opened – but Ron still managed to persuade the customers that this was perfectly normal. We had sold somewhere between twenty to thirty of these foul creatures before the market's manager arrived, condemned our entire stock & ordered all remaining crabs to be destroyed. Sorry if that story has given you indigestion – if it's any consolation, I haven't eaten crab from that day to this.

'I Scrubbed the Crabs that Killed Sheffield' was my attempt to tell this unfortunate story in song. What *did* happen to the people who ate those tainted crabs? Is it too late to apologise to them? Even though, as I said, I was only following orders?

This song, ridiculous as it is, is my very first attempt to find a 'third way' in my songwriting. Trying to steer a path between the twin pillars of flippant jokiness on the one hand & dire over-earnestness on the other.

Mr. & Mrs. W. Hoyland
request the pleasure of the company of

....

at the marriage of their daughter
Christine
with Mr. George Malcolm Cocker
at St. Cyprian's Church Frecheville
Wednesday, April 24th, 1963, at 5-0 p.m
and afterwards at the Embassy Ballroom, Mansfield Road,
Sheffield, 12.

R.S.V.P.   122, MANSFIELD ROAD,
                                                      SHEFFIELD, 12

There was a more recent example of 'real life' in the lyric of 'Little Girl (With Blue Eyes)'. The title track of the record we had just released.

I had been looking through a drawer in my mum's house one day & found the wedding photo opposite. It really affected me. The look on my mother's face is what really made an impression. She looks very young. & she looks very scared.

Everyone's interested to see pictures of their mums & dads on the 'big day' – we kid ourselves we can see the beginnings of our own life story in those awkwardly posed official photographs – but I was slightly more . . . involved in my parents' wedding day than is the norm. How can I put it? I was there.

My mum was twenty-one years old at the time she got married. She had gone to the doctor's with an abdominal pain & was informed that she was four months' pregnant. This came as a shock to her as she wasn't in a relationship at the time & hadn't been for a while. The necessary maths was done & my conception was traced back to a party around the previous Christmas holidays. My father was located & informed. The relationship between him & my mother had only lasted a month & they hadn't seen each other since but, back in those days, the 'right thing to do' under the circumstances was for the two of them to get married. & that's exactly what happened on Wednesday 24 April 1963.

Little girl with blue eyes
there's a hole in your heart
& one between your legs
you've never had to wonder
which one he's going to fill
in spite of what he said.

Thus ran the chorus of the song the wedding photograph inspired me to write. I wrote the words to 'Little Girl . . .' when I was the same age my mum had been when she got married.

Twenty-one going on twenty-two. But, whereas I was still at the very beginning of my creative life, my arrival had brought hers to an abrupt end: she'd been two years into a Fine Art degree at Sheffield's Psalter Lane Art College when she was forced to drop out to attend to her motherly responsibilities. Sorry, Mum.

That's quite a lot to process at any age. & the song is my attempt to deal with this information. I don't think it's a coincidence that I wrote it when we were the same age – I was measuring my experience against my mother's & taking note of the difference. Using words to try to fill the hole in my own heart. (That's another thing creativity can do for you – you can repair yourself. Or at least have a good try.)

This concept of songwriting as self-help/therapy is a lovely idea, but the immediate impact of the lyrics to this song was that our single got banned by the local radio station in Sheffield. As the article 'Cocker Comes a Cropper' puts it: 'They have also ran [sic] into problems with radio play for the single – one Radio Hallam deejay faded it out when he heard the chorus, and that was at one a.m.' The glorious Second Coming of Pulp was on the rocks. Mainly due to my navigation.

'The blow has come at a crucial time for the band who have just released their Little Girl (With Blue Eyes) single and were due to play an important date at the Greyhound in London on December 11. Unless Cocker undergoes a miracle recovery this date looks almost certain to be cancelled.' I'm starting to think the *Star* got their sports reporter to write this article. But hold on a minute. It's only now, decades later, as I re-read 'Cocker Comes a Cropper' that I realise I have been committing another significant act of mis-remembering: I've always told myself that the fall from the window took place in the run-up to the release of the 'Little Girl' EP, that it was an unfortunate incident that prevented the single from realising its full potential – but the newspaper specifically states that the record is already out in the world. & bombing.

ILFORD HP5

▲ 28A

28

▲ 27A

It gets stranger. Take a look at this photo, another out-take from the session to find a cover image for the 'Little Girl' EP. I'm lying on the floor wearing the same clothes I fell out of the window in.*

What to make of this dress-rehearsal photo? Premonition or coincidence? Plastic tortoise or red herring? Once again we're dealing with a fact: this is photographic evidence. Could I really have had some inkling of the disaster that was about to befall me? Well, how about we make another new pile? A TRUTH IS STRANGER THAN FICTION pile?

Post-accident, I now felt I could amend this time-honoured phrase: it turned out truth was not only stranger than fiction.

It was infinitely more interesting.

* OK, maybe that's a stretch ... but I'm definitely wearing the same boots – they're visible in the 'smooth' stool photo (page 298). They were a pair of black zip-up patent-leather boots I was particularly proud of but which were two sizes too big & so did absolutely nothing to protect the ankle that took the brunt of the impact when I plummeted to the ground. I remember a doctor telling me that when I was in hospital. I thought he was about to prescribe me some sensible brogues or something.

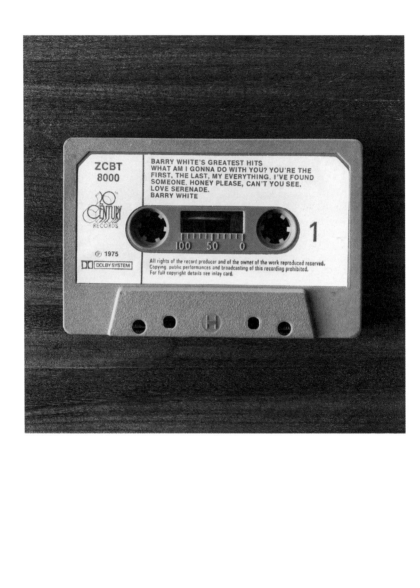

Chapter Twenty-Three

We have unearthed more gold –
White Gold!

You've just seen a cassette copy of *Barry White's Greatest Hits* released in 1975 on 20th Century Records. Very nice sage-green plastic tape housing. This is definitely a KEEPer. Can't wait to play it again. Barry White is one of my major musical influences.

I listened to this cassette a lot when I was in hospital recovering from the fall. I didn't own a Walkman at the time but someone lent me one to help me while away the bed-bound hours. This cassette originally belonged to Russell's mum. (Wonder if she'd like it back?) Anyway, it's a very good 'in' to the story of how Russell & I fell head over heels in love with Barry White . . .

Not long after the current line-up of Pulp had first got together, Russell began trying his hand at the antiques trade. He'd just completed a Business Studies degree at university so I guess he wanted to put what he'd learnt into practice. He asked if I'd like to get involved. He knew that my bedroom at The Wicker was stuffed full of jumble sale purchases – I had already accumulated some 'capital', as he might have put it.

I'd never really thought about the things I was buying at jumble sales as having any value beyond that which I'd assigned them. That was something else I really liked about the Jumble Life – it felt like you were bucking the system in some way; living on the cast-offs of the consumer society meant you couldn't be a victim of it. I was a Second-Hand Outlaw. A Recycled Renegade.

But utopias never last. Dealers eventually cottoned on to what was happening & started turning up to jumble sales in droves. There was a guy who had a second-hand clothes shop in the city centre ('vintage clothing' wasn't a common phrase yet) & my heart would sink when I saw him in front of me in the queue because I knew he would hoover up all the decent men's clothes before I could get a look-in. Sometimes he would even jump the queue by offering the church that was holding the sale £50 if they let him in an hour before the doors opened to the public. That's cheating! (I guess others would call it 'Entrepreneurship'.) Cast him out of the temple! But the ongoing recession in Sheffield meant that nothing was sacred. Everyone was scrabbling about for cash wherever they could find it.

Russell took me on a trip to an auction in a place called Thurcroft in an attempt to whet my appetite for the antiques trade. This is the point at which Barry White enters our story. Russell had the use of his mother's minivan for this trip. It was a strange vehicle – from a distance it looked like a normal white transit van but when you were standing next to it you realised it was only about two-thirds the size. It was as though a mad scientist had shrunk it with a magic ray gun. & the metal it was made out of was thinner than standard too – it felt very much like you were travelling in a tin can on wheels. Maximum speed was 50 mph because – you guessed it – the engine was also smaller than average.

All these factors combined to make travelling in this van an uncomfortable & extremely noisy experience. Especially when you were going uphill. & as Sheffield is built on seven hills there was never much respite from the tortured mechanical grinding sounds coming from under the hood.

We attempted to drown out this din by turning up the radio cassette player fitted in the van but the aerial had fallen off & the eject button on the cassette player wasn't working. So we had no choice but to listen to the tape trapped in the player. That meant side 1 of *Barry White's Greatest Hits* for the entire journey. Thank you, universe!

Of course, I'd heard Barry White before – my pop addiction meant I was aware of him – but only now did I fall deeply in love with his music. There's something so open & joyous about it. It's danceable but also really lush. You can lie back & relax in it. Barry's got things covered. He's got your back. The tunes are great but I also really liked the sections where he stopped singing just to talk for a while. Although not as rhythmically defined as rap, his delivery dovetails perfectly with the musical backing – he makes it seem effortless. Barry is smooth. To say I was impressed would be an understatement. Every time the tape reached the end of the side we rewound it & listened all over again. & our respect & reverence grew. By the time we reached our destination we were both looking at each other & saying, 'We have to make music like this!'*

We arrived at the auction in Thurcroft a little late & so had limited time to view the upcoming lots. The bulk of which appeared to be plastic storage boxes filled with random items. I don't use the word 'random' lightly: a typical box might contain a fish slice, three unmatched plates, a dog toy, two raffia table mats & a roll of Sellotape. The boxes were strewn around the warehouse, each with a number felt-tipped on its side. There must have been about a hundred of them in all.

Sotheby's it was not.

The auctioneer was also nothing like the ones I'd seen on TV. He had a broad South Yorkshire accent & was telling the crowd to settle down in no uncertain terms. He gave one final 'Shut it!' over the rudimentary PA system & the sale of the century got under way.

'Lot One – who'll give me ten?'

Someone on the front row twitched.

'All right – do I hear twenty?'

A cough from elsewhere in the room.

I couldn't believe it – twenty quid for a box full of garbage? This auction lark might be worth getting involved in after all!

The price kept going up.

'Eighty.'

'Ninety.'

* We were true to our word: there's a Pulp song called 'My Legendary Girlfriend' that basically combines the music from 'Honey Please, Can't Ya See' (Track 4, Side 1) with the vocal approach of 'Love Serenade' (Track 5, Side 1). Though it wasn't released until 1991, the song had been a staple of our live set since 1986. Thank you, Barry.

What the hell was going on? It didn't make any sense whatsoever.

& then the auctioneer uttered a phrase that will for ever be etched upon my memory:

'Cap's in at a pound.'

Allow me to translate – the man in the flat cap standing in the centre of the room has just raised the bidding to the princely sum of . . . £1.

THEY HAD BEEN BIDDING IN PENCE!

A room full of grown men bidding in 10p increments on boxes filled with crap. That kind of sums up Sheffield in the mid '80s for me.

Down came the hammer at £1.20 (quite literally: the auctioneer was holding a claw hammer rather than the traditional gavel) & then the whole process began again for Lot Two. It was hypnotic. Russell & I didn't stay for the entire auction but nothing went for more than £2 during the time we were there. By then I knew that the life of an antique dealer was not for me. I had enjoyed the 'performance art' aspect of what we'd just witnessed but I couldn't imagine myself being one of the 'performers' myself. & besides, we'd already unearthed a treasure beyond our wildest dreams on the journey over: we'd discovered Barry White.

PEOPLE I HAVE MET WHILST IN HOSPITAL

① DOUG #1 - ABOUT 50, TRAPPED NERVE, ALWAYS GIVING NURSES QUALITY STREET, SILLY SHOES WITH HIGHISH HEELS. HIT BY TAXI, TEETH REMOVED TO FIX SHO-

② HANDY MAN - FUNNY SMILE, KEPT GOING OFF FOR A FAG, THEN WHEN IMMOBILE SNEAKED THE ODD ONE IN THE WARD EVEN THOUGH HE HAD A CHEST INFECTION. LOADS OF RELATIVES, FAT YOUNG WIFE.

③ ERNEST - OLD, V. THIN, ON TRACTION, KEPT MOVING WHEN HE SHOULDN'T HAVE & EXPOSING HIMSELF. HAD BAD CHEST. COULDN'T TALK PROPERLY KIND OF GROAN. LET OUT HORRIBLE GURGLING COUGH AND GROANS ALL DAY & NIGHT. GRADUALLY GOT QUIETER AS TIME WENT ON. ONE NIGHT A LOT OF ACTIVITY, PUT HIM ON OXYGEN BUT IN THE MORNING HE HAD DIED. WE WERE ALL MOV- TO THE DAY ROOM UNTIL HIS RELATIVES HAD BEE- TO SEE THE BODY.

④ TOWNIE-TASH MAN - MOVED INTO ERNEST'S BED. BIT OF A POSER. HAD TIGHT-FITTING PYJAMAS W- TROUSER LEGS ROLLED UP & TOP TUCKED IN.

⑤ MR. McCONE - TOTALLY PATHETIC & DEPRESSING, ON THE WARD I WAS MOVED TO. HICCUPED CONSTANTL- SHAT HIMSELF EVERY MORNING (I HAD TO ASK FOR

332

A NOSEGAY BECAUSE THE STINK WAS SO BAD) HAD A
BOWEL OPERATION WHICH HAD GONE WRONG. CALLED
ALL DOCTORS "SIR" & CURTSEYED TO THE NURSES. THREW
UP ONE NIGHT. HAD A BAG FITTED & WALKED
AROUND WITH IT HANGING FOR ALL TO SEE. TOTAL
WASTE OF TIME.

⑥ MR WHITE-HAIR CONKY — SIMILAR TO McCOUE
BUT NOT QUITE AS BAD. FARTED CONSTANTLY
WORE PAPER KNICKERS & HAD HIS PRICK
ALL BANDAGED UP.

⑦ BRUNO — ON F2. POLISH I THINK. CALLED
ALL THE NURSES "BABYCHAM" ALWAYS ORDERING
NURSES ABOUT, GETTING THEM TO WHEEL HIM SO
DAYROOM ETC. SMOKED IN WARD. APPARANTLY
THE MAN WITH THE MOST DRINK-DRIVING CONVICTIONS
IN SHEFFIELD. FUNNY.

⑧ DOUG #2 — WATER-VOLE MAN. REPEATED EACH
STORY AT LEAST 5 TIMES. A NYTHERER.
WIFE LOOKED LIKE A LABRADOR. GREAT FRIENDS
WITH GEORGE (SEE BELOW)

⑨ GEORGE — THE BOSS OF KING EDWARDS. IN FOR
HIS HIP FUSION, HAS BEEN IN MANY MONTHS.
KNOWS EVERYONE, ALWAYS JOKING, BRINGS SALT
& PEPPER ROUND AT MEAL-TIMES. WOULD BE
A GOOD REP-CONT.

ALL THE KIDS SINGING THE CAROLS &
4 4-15 YEAR OLD GIRLS ON <3 WITH THE
PROPER LONG-LEGGED SATIN LEOTARDS ON, THE
OTHER COULD ONLY MANAGE STRETCH (DENIMS)
DOING DISCO DANCING TO "LA BAMBA" (KNOWN
AS "CARAMBA, CARAMBA" DOWN AT OUR END OF
THE WARD) WITH VERY LITTLE ENTHUSIASM
OR STYLE, BUT IT WERE A RIGHT LAUGH.

PEOPLE (CONTD.)

HEINRICH:- A POLISH MAN. GOOD ACCENT; CALLS
PHYSIOTHERAPY "FEEZIO". LOOKS SLAVIC. (THICK
SET BUT NOT IN THE SOFT FLABBY ENGLISH WAY, MORE
LIKE A LUMP OF STONE) HAD A KNACKERED IN
ARTIFICIAL HIP BUT HAD TO WAIT TWO YEARS FOR
TREATMENT. CONSEQUENCE:- NOW HAS NO HIP AT ALL
AND THAT LEG IS ABOUT 2TWO 3 INCHES SHORTER
THAN THE OTHER.

KEITH - BIG, BELLYISH, GLASSES, ADMITTED TO
K.E. VII SAME DAY AS ME. LOOKS LIKE A
FAT MARC RILEY. ON TRACTION. FRIEND OF
GEORGE'S. BROUGHT A "BROAD-MINDED" TAPE FOR ME
TO LISTEN TO. CONSTIPATED FOR AGES. BIT OF A
MILD-MANNERED MOANER. LEFT EARLY BECAUSE OF
HOME PROBLEMS.

I didn't spend all my time in hospital listening to Barry White on a borrowed Walkman. I had work to do. I was keen to start applying the insights I'd gained after my fall from the window. I'd been observing my surroundings in the hospital in as much detail as possible. I was taking My Revelation very seriously – as you can see from the three sheets of paper reproduced on the previous pages, where I have written descriptions of 'People I Have Met Whilst in Hospital'. KEEP.

First up is 'Doug #1': 'Doug #1 – about fifty – trapped nerve – always giving the nurses Quality Street – silly shoes with highish heels – hit by a taxi – teeth removed to fix skull.'

It reads like the notes a private detective might make whilst tailing a suspect – & in a way that's exactly what they are. From now on I was going to note every detail of the world around me, hoping to stumble across a clue that would crack the whole case wide open. & who knew what that vital clue might turn out to be? Could it be the fact that Doug #1 gave the nurses Quality Street rather than another chocolate/toffee assortment? Or would following the footprints left by his 'silly shoes with highish heels' guide me to the truth I was seeking? I had no way of knowing – &, to be honest, I didn't know exactly what it was I was seeking either – but I was now possessed by the unshakeable belief that if only I could capture what was happening around me accurately enough then it would all make sense in the end.

Plus, working undercover was fun.

The investigation really gained momentum after I was transferred from the Royal Hallamshire Hospital to the King Edward VII Convalescent Hospital. At the Hallamshire I had been in a room containing three other beds, the occupants of which changed from day to day. In the case of Ernest (suspect #3 on my list) it was because he died during the night. Suspects #5 ('Mr McCone') & #6 ('Mr White-Hair Conky' – perhaps not his birth name) were transferred to other hospital departments once they were out of any danger. This quick turnover meant I never got to know anyone in depth. The King Edward VII Convalescent

Hospital, on the other hand, was – as the name implies – a place where patients were sent to recover over a period of time. That not only meant I was well on the road to recovery, it also gave me the chance to really 'embed' myself.

Meet 'George' (#9 on my list). My description of George reads: 'The "Boss" of King Edward's – in for hip fusing – has been in many months – knows everything – always joking – brings salt & pepper round at meal-times – would be a good Red Coat.'

George welcomed me to the hospital & introduced me to the other men on the ward. I appreciated him doing that – it helped me feel less awkward. It also dispelled any feelings of self-pity I might have been harbouring: I had now been hospitalised for a fortnight & was due to spend another month recovering here, which felt like a long time to be out of action to me, but there were guys in King Edward's who'd been convalescing far longer than that. Bruno (suspect #7: 'Polish – calls all the nurses "Babycham" – apparently the man with the most drink-driving convictions in Sheffield') had done six months already & was due to remain for another eight, while recovering from a mining accident. My 'sentence' was piddling compared to that.

&, at twenty-two I was by far the youngest patient on the ward. I was hanging out with men from a different generation. & with very different backgrounds to mine: these guys had jobs, for a start! In fact, most of them were there due to work-related accidents (let that be a lesson to you). Talking to them was an education.

Take Bruno: Bruno was a miner. The miners' strike had finished earlier that year. Over the course of twelve months Margaret Thatcher succeeded in destroying the strongest trade union in the UK. Russell had been very supportive of the strike – he'd gone on pickets & had covered his guitar in 'Coal Not Dole' stickers. I'd been more ambivalent. Mainly because I equated miners with 'townies'.

Townies were the bane of your life if you looked alternative in Sheffield in the '80s. That's why weirdos stuck to drinking in the Hallamshire Hotel & dancing in The Limit (both on West Street): if you strayed into other parts of town you got beaten up. Absolutely guaranteed. I had a special route that I took to get from The Wicker to West Street without passing through any townie strongholds. I used to imagine that I was in a giant game of Pac-Man trying to evade those funny blobby things (ghosts?) that follow you & block your way & eventually kill you if you're not careful. I did pretty well (especially compared to someone like General Dyson, who I mentioned earlier) but I didn't get off completely scot-free. I've still got a faint scar on my forehead from when a bunch of football hooligans rampaged through the Hallamshire one night & started throwing beer glasses around whilst bellowing, 'Yellows!' I was the last person to duck (my slow reflexes yet again) & took a pint pot to the head. It looked very dramatic because cuts to the forehead bleed profusely. The landlord gave me a free drink to calm my nerves – only free drink I ever got in that place.

My worst encounter with townie violence, however, was undoubtedly the time I got 'kebabbed'. I was waiting outside the cathedral for the night bus back to my mum's house after a night at The Limit. A group of townies walked by & started taking the piss out of my clothes. Specifically a black patent mac I was wearing. 'Look at that sack of rubbish out on the pavement,' said one wag. (I think he was implying that my coat resembled a bin bag.) They carried on taunting me but I refused to take the bait seeing as I was on my own & there were seven of them. The bus eventually arrived. I got on & sat downstairs towards the rear. The townies were still making faces & giving me the rods from outside. Emboldened by being in the safety of the bus I also stuck two fingers up & mouthed, 'Fuck you!' through the window. Big mistake. I'd forgotten that night buses waited at their stands outside the cathedral for ten minutes before setting off. That gave late-night revellers a bit of leeway when drunkenly making their way from club to bus stop. I saw the ringleader of the gang approach the front door of the bus. He exchanged some words with the driver & then began walking down the aisle towards me. Shit. The look on his face was not friendly.

When he got to where I was sitting he stopped & said, 'Here, I've got something for you,' & produced a half-eaten kebab from behind his back – which he then pushed into my face with considerable force. Having made his delivery he turned on his heel & left the bus. His mates outside were pissing themselves. I was trying my best to make like nothing had happened. The other passengers on the bottom deck all turned round to stare. Being kebabbed didn't hurt as much as the pint glass to the head but it was far more humiliating. I had to sit for the entire journey home covered in bits of shredded cabbage & foul-smelling meat. Still, looking on the bright side, at least the patent mac the townies had found so amusing in the first place was wipe-clean.

Events like this naturally made me wary of townies. In fact, the constant threat of violence made me avoid them like the plague. But there was no avoiding Bruno – he was in the bed next to me – & speaking to him & Keith (#11 on the list: 'Big, bellyish, glasses – on traction – looks like a fat Marc Riley'), another miner recovering from an accident, made me realise that I'd been guilty of making a blanket judgement. Categorising all miners as townies was just wrong. I'd had a couple of bad experiences that led to me seeing the situation in black-&-white terms. I don't want to get all 'Ebony & Ivory' on you here but there really *is* 'good & bad in everyone'. Good miners, bad miners, good indie weirdos, bad indie weirdos. Maybe even good townies, bad townies. (Good pop, bad pop.) Once you start looking at things *in detail* you can't help but see that the world is a far more nuanced place than it might first appear. Try it. You'll realise there is no Us & Them – just many, many different varieties of Us.

This new-found, blissed-out, loved-up respect for all my

fellow human beings was put to the test almost immediately by Keith (recovering miner #2).

The key line in the character assessment of Keith I wrote is: 'Brought a "broad-minded" tape for me to listen to.'

Keith made me listen to Roy 'Chubby' Brown.

For the uninitiated, Roy 'Chubby' Brown is 'an English stand-up comedian whose act consists of offensive humour, high profanity, forthright social commentary & outspoken disdain for political correctness'.* He had a big hit back in 1995 with 'Living Next Door to Alice (Who the Fuck is Alice?)'. Surely you remember that one? Keith was obviously expecting a right-on Leftie like me to hate Roy 'Chubby' Brown.

The ward at King Edward's was long & thin & the beds were arranged in two rows that ran the length of the walls facing each other. There were twenty beds in all. The Roy 'Chubby' Brown virus slowly worked its way through the room, passing from bed to bed. Keith gave his Walkman to his neighbour who duly listened to it & passed it to the occupant of the next bed & so on. I was second-to-last in line. The wait was excruciating. All the other guys were guffawing as soon as they put the headphones on – what if I just didn't find it funny at all? Would they all fall out with me? I didn't want to lose my new friends – but I certainly wasn't going to laugh along to something really vile & nasty. The Walkman reached my bed & all eyes were on me . . .

In the end I laughed twice: once at a joke the punchline of which was, 'Excuse me, could you pass the fanny?' & then again at a description of an overnight stay he & his wife made at a hotel in France which began: 'We had a Continental Breakfast – ate the quilt.' Phew. Challenge successfully completed.

---

* According to Wikipedia.

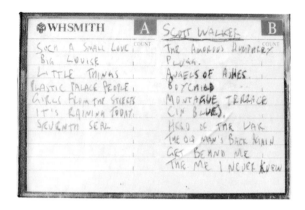

I got my own back on Keith a couple of days later by making him listen to Scott Walker.

I'm glad we found this cassette up here in the loft because listening to this compilation is how I first discovered Scott Walker's music – music that has been very precious to me throughout my life. For that reason it goes in the KEEP pile. This is where a lifelong relationship began.

Although that's my handwriting on the cassette inlay, I'd been given the tape by a friend some six months before my accident. I can't remember who though. Isn't that strange? Your life is changed for ever for the better & you don't even know who to thank for it. I think he had blonde hair.

I'll thank Julian Cope instead: because this cassette is a copy of *Fire Escape in the Sky: The Godlike Genius of Scott Walker*, an album of music taken from Scott's late- '6os solo albums that Cope compiled for Zoo Records in 1981. Julian Cope conceived of this album as a way of introducing Scott Walker's music to a new post-punk audience – of presenting it in such a way that they wouldn't feel they were buying into 'some dodgy '6os MOR icon' (his words, not mine). I was precisely the demographic he was aiming at. I'd heard the hits Scott had enjoyed as a member of The Walker Brothers & I'd even bought an album from a jumble sale called *Scott Walker – The Moviegoer*, which featured him singing famous film themes, but I didn't have him marked down as a Major Artist. All that changed when I listened to this cassette.

I was in bed in The Wicker with a case of flu (again) when I remembered I'd been given this tape a few days earlier. I crawled out of bed to locate it, then put it in the tape player & pressed 'Play'. I was feverish & the music swished around my mind as I drifted in & out of consciousness. Things started to get weird during Track 4, Side 1, 'Plastic Palace People'. I just couldn't work out whether I was awake or asleep. There was some swirling orchestral music that made me feel like I was flying & then someone started singing about a balloon in polka-dot underwear. That couldn't be right, could it? Then the song went into a harsh, atonal section – the singing became all echoey & strange like in a horror film. Then the flying music started all over again. The song seemed to go on like this for ever, repeating the same sections over & over again. Real songs don't do that, do they? This couldn't be happening – I must have just had too much cough mixture.

But I hadn't. Scott Walker was singing about stray balloons, lonely transvestites, plane crashes, people being swallowed by the telly, other people worried that a fat man in the flat above was going to crash through their ceiling any minute, backed by the most sumptuous, widescreen, orchestral music you ever heard in your life. It was the 'epic in the everyday' made audible.

Thank you, Julian Cope. Thank you, nameless blonde acquaintance from Sheffield. Ever since that bout of flu I'd been listening to this cassette obsessively – so I asked Tim to bring it into hospital for me. It felt even more pertinent to listen to it now in light of My Revelation.

Keith's verdict was that Scott's singing sounded 'a bit like Andy Williams'.

Here's my favourite button on the
Yamaha PortaSound PS-400:

the
DISCO
button!

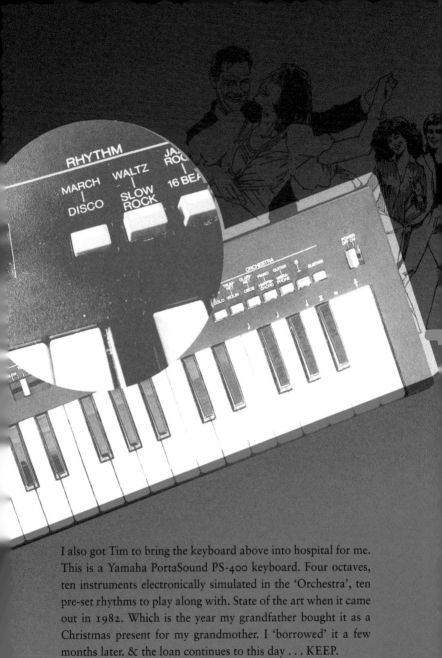

I also got Tim to bring the keyboard above into hospital for me. This is a Yamaha PortaSound PS-400 keyboard. Four octaves, ten instruments electronically simulated in the 'Orchestra', ten pre-set rhythms to play along with. State of the art when it came out in 1982. Which is the year my grandfather bought it as a Christmas present for my grandmother. I 'borrowed' it a few months later. & the loan continues to this day . . . KEEP.

I wanted to be able to write songs whilst in hospital but there was no way I was going to lie there strumming away on an acoustic guitar in front of all the other guys on the ward. (That old fear of being overheard again.) So this seemed the perfect solution. It's got a headphone socket, meaning creative privacy is ensured. Good outcome for all concerned if you ask me. (Remember Guantánamo.)

I missed playing with the band & this was the nearest I could get. If you depress the AUTO-CHORD ACCOMPANIMENT button (with the RHYTHM SECTION activated) then it's almost like having a band at your fingertips. (With the added bonus that they don't complain if you ask them to play the same riff for ten minutes.)

My favourite button on the Yamaha PortaSound PS-400 is at the extreme left of the rhythm section: the DISCO button!

Press any key on the lowest octave of the keyboard & you instantly have a full band playing a basic, four-to-the-floor disco groove. I loved it. At last I could try to write music like the stuff I'd been dancing to in The Limit all these years. I wrote many songs using that one setting. It's like that when you find a new instrument: it unlocks fresh possibilities. Together with my discovery of Barry White this keyboard sent my songwriting off in a new direction. I first attempted to make dance music, the music of the human body, whilst confined to bed in a convalescent hospital. I would stay up late into the night, propped up on pillows, writing music for an imaginary dance floor that I would be physically unable to 'strut my stuff' on for quite some time.

Although my customary nightlife routine of two trips to The Limit per week had been curtailed, I did manage to get in a couple of visits to the cinema. Or rather, the cinema came to me. Every other Thursday a man would come and set his 16mm film projector up at one end of the ward & a screen at the other. Then the beds were wheeled round to form 'rows', the lights dimmed & that evening's feature would begin. It was a magical experience – made even more magical by the fact there were no televisions on the ward – this was our sole fortnightly exposure to moving images.

Not that the films shown were masterpieces of cinematic art. First up was *The Cannonball Run*. The guys liked the car chases. The choice of picture a fortnight later was more puzzling. *Star 80* starring Mariel Hemingway – a film based on the true-life story of Dorothy Stratten, a *Playboy* centrefold who was murdered by her boyfriend (spoiler). It wasn't a porn film but, given the subject matter, it was hardly surprising that it did feature a fair amount of nudity. 'Hands visible on top of the covers, lads!' shouted George, assuming responsibility for our moral well-being. It was like being in a scene from a *Carry On* film.

Something very important was happening to me whilst in hospital. A Convalescence & also a Coalescence. A magic formula was brewing. If I had to chalk it up on a blackboard it would read:

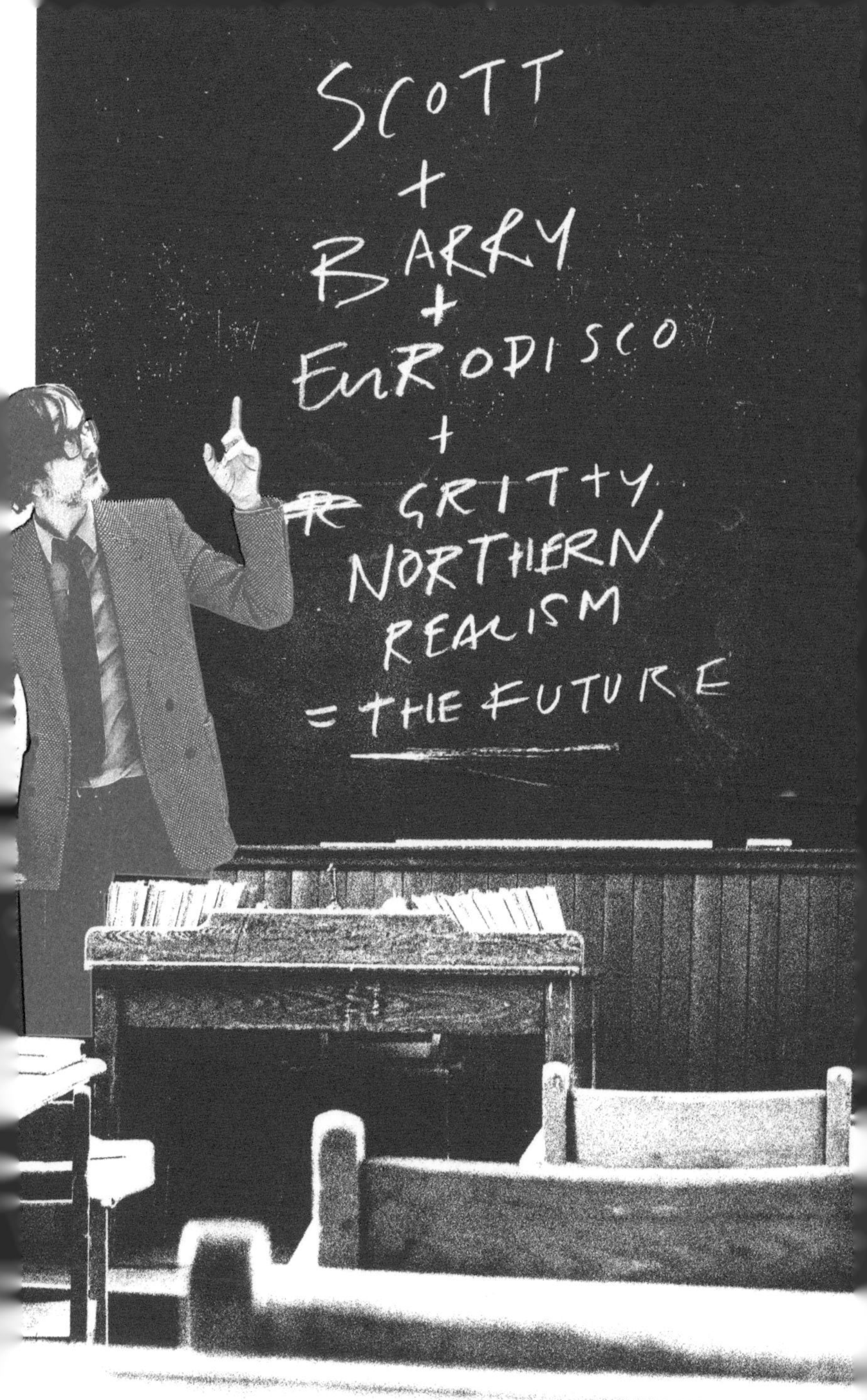
SCOTT
+
BARRY
+
EURODISCO
+
GRITTY
NORTHERN
REALISM
= THE FUTURE

There was loads of other stuff in the equation too. If it could be represented in visual terms it would probably resemble the contents of this loft: a jumble of things with no one factor in dominance – it's the mix that's important. Seemingly inconsequential items can end up having long-term effects if added to the mix in the right quantities.

& now the fall from the window had shaken up all this stuff & blended it together. A chain reaction had been set in motion. I felt on the verge of a major life-changing breakthrough. (& no, I wasn't still on powerful pain medication.)

I was due to leave King Edward's the day before Christmas Eve. In the meantime I was given lessons in using crutches & how to control a wheelchair. I wouldn't be fully mobile for another month yet but I could continue my recovery in the civilian world so long as I moved back to my mum's house. The doctor was very insistent about that. I'd had a chest infection that almost developed into pneumonia during my first weeks in hospital. The doctor asked whether I'd been living in a cold, damp, dirty environment. I described my bedroom at The Wicker & that seemed to tick all those particular boxes. He told me in no uncertain terms not to return there or I would run a real risk of getting a full-blown lung condition. The end of an era – by medical decree.

I got dressed in civilian clothes for the first time in almost two months & waited for Tim to pick me up in his van & drive me to my mum's. I put on the coat pictured opposite. I was taking the doctor's advice to keep warm seriously. This is a black fake-fur coat designed by Hardy Amies for Hepworths.

Very warm, very snuggly. & very precious. I inherited this coat from my grandfather after he died in 1983. I remember him picking me up in it when I was a kid & pretending that he was a bear. I really believed it at the time. Now it was my turn to be Poppa Bear. That suited me just fine. KEEP.

As I was sitting on my bed awaiting Tim's arrival, a group

of local schoolkids turned up to do a Christmas show for the patients. They assembled at the far end of the ward near the Christmas tree. First the younger kids sang carols in that gleefuly, atonal manner that only pre-teens can pull off convincingly. Then four slightly older girls treated us to a dance routine they'd worked out to 'La Bamba' (which Bruno insisted on calling 'Caramba Caramba'). Three of the girls were wearing golden leotards with matching leggings whilst the remaining dancer obviously hadn't received the memo & was wearing a vest tucked into a pair of stretch jeans. I found their combined lack of enthusiasm at having to perform to a roomful of old codgers extremely amusing. I was in love with the whole world at that moment. I was going home, I was going to be all right – & it was Christmas! Finally the scriptwriter was back on board.

Tim arrived & carried my things to the van. I followed behind him, swaying on my crutches. The guys all shouted, 'Merry Christmas!' as I left the room. I paused just beyond the front doors of the hospital & felt the movement of air on my face. It was my first time outside in two months. I took a deep breath & stood in the car park looking down on the street lights of Sheffield glittering in the dark. Twinkling a welcome. Welcome home. I was back from the brink. Out of the tunnel. Wrapped up warm in my grandad's old coat & ready to embark on the next leg of the adventure.

Tim started the engine of the van & I manoeuvred myself into the passenger seat.

It was time to go.

Central School of Art and Design

Southampton Row London WC1B 4AP Telephone 01-405 1825

Head of School: D.C.Sherlock BA MPhil MSDI FRSA

Administration

Dear Mr Cockes,

COUNCIL FOR NATIONAL ACEDEMIC AWARDS –
REGISTRATION SCHEME 1988/89
ADMISSIONS TO FIRST DEGREE COURSES IN ART AND DESIGN

I am pleased to inform you that your application for admission to
the degree course in FA – Film + Video   has been successful.

You are requested to confirm or decline our offer of a place as
soon as possible by completing the Form of Declaration overleaf.

From September 1988, the Central School will join St Martin's
School of Art to form a new, merged college. It will be called
Central and St Martin's School of Art and Design and will
therefore preserve all the advantages of public reputation built
up over many years. The range of courses of the two existing
colleges are complementary and we expect only improvements in the
facilities and opportunities available to you as a result of the
merger. The new college will have about 1,400 students and
probably the most comprehensive range of undergraduate and
postgraduate courses in art and design in the country.

The course commences on Monday 26 September 1988 and you should
attend at 9.30 a.m. on that day. On arrival you will be asked to
pay your fees or produce written evidence that your Education
Authority or some other body will pay them, <u>otherwise enrolment
for the course may be refused.</u>

Students are expected to make their own arrangements for
accommodation well before the beginning of the session. A
booklet entitled "Handbook on Student Services", prepared by the
Student Counsellor, is enclosed, which she hopes you will find
useful.

<u>Fine Art students</u>

Please understand that you will be enrolled at the Central School
<u>not</u> St Martin's. Please ensure that in any correspondence with
your local authority this is made clear.

Yours sincerely

R Cegau

Registrar

26 × 45.70

5%

= 45.70   13/400
  × 26   39400
  39620   270820
  13 1400
  52 5.9600

Epilogue

I'd love to be able to tell you that, armed with my newly defined creative vision, I walked out of hospital, straight into one of the top art colleges in the country & ran slap bang into the subject matter of The Song That Made My Name – but it didn't happen like that. This acceptance letter from St Martin's School of Art didn't arrive until two & a half years later. But it was in the post.

As soon as I got out of hospital I knew that my days in Sheffield were numbered. During the drive to my mum's, Tim told me that a mutual acquaintance, Dave Loukes – singer with a local band called Quite Unnerving – had died the previous week after falling off a motorbike. Living in Sheffield was starting to feel like being one of those Agatha Christie novels where the characters get bumped off one by one. If I hung around much longer I too would come to a sticky end. I'd just had a lucky escape & had to learn from that.

But these things take time. It's been like that up here in the loft: when we started I assumed we'd get it tidied in one go, but this feels like a good place to take a break – I've just had a near-death experience & simultaneously located my creative vision: think we've earned a breather.

I'm going to leave you with a bit of bling. During The Wicker years I stored my jewellery in this plastic apple which stood next to the depressing ballerina alarm clock.

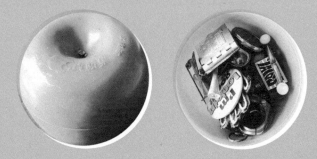

No hallmarks or anything: all jumble-sale finds. Assorted odd cufflinks, a weird Victorian contraption that holds your shirt collars together (maybe that's why I've never needed collar supports), a few rings & brooches. But what I really wanted to show you is a tiny book.

I've placed a 1p coin next to the book to show just how tiny it really is. This is a book of tattoos (or 'TATOOS' as it's spelt on the cover) & it is a very precious, very Pop item. It came from a bubblegum machine.

There was a bubblegum machine, like the one pictured above,* outside the sweet shop on our road. Unlike the one above though, it had a small number of 'TATOO' books distributed amongst the gumballs. You could see them through the glass panels on the front of the machine. Tantalising.

Every day I would put my 1p in the slot, turn the handle, hear the distinctive ping of a gumball falling into the delivery chute & then carefully lift the metal flap, not wishing my gumball to fall on to the ground & get dirty. Then I would crouch down & closely inspect the delivery area, hoping against hope that I would find one of the 'TATOO' books in there as well. The bubblegum was horrible: it would crumble into a sticky powder when you tried to chew it. I suspect some of those gumballs had been in there for years. The 'TATOO' books were the real prize you were hoping for every time you put a coin in the slot.

* I took this photo in Berlin recently.

I walked past the bubblegum machine twice a day on my way to & from school. If I had a penny on me I would always give it a try – to no avail.

This went on all the way through Infants & Juniors. Then, one day, the unthinkable happened. I lifted the metal flap & this book was lying there. I could not believe my eyes.

You take a page from the book, place it face down on a part of your body, wet it, leave it for a few seconds & then, when you peel it off, Hey Presto! you've got a tattoo. But of course I couldn't bring myself to do that.

This book seemed far too precious for me to destroy it that way. So I kept it in a safe place for years. Inside a plastic apple.

I'd already been indelibly marked by pop anyway. I didn't need a tattoo to prove it.

This book was of more use to me intact – as a reminder that dreams do come true. If you're prepared to wait long enough.

This was an important message to keep in mind – especially later, during the darkest days of the Th*tcher Years. There's always a way out.

This is really a tiny book of magic spells to protect me from Bad Pop. KEEP.

The other way I warded off the Bad Pop was, of course, by writing songs. Until I wrote this book the only way I've ever tried to detail my passage through life has been through songs. I haven't gone into too much detail in this book about specific songs I have written. That *would* be violating the terms of the Magic Circle & I'd be blatantly messing with the 'sacred mechanics' that Leonard Cohen referred to during our interview in 2012.
    HOWEVER ...

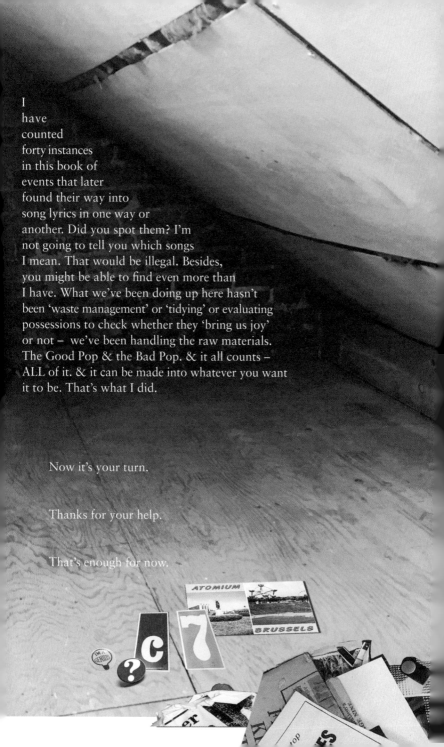

I
have
counted
forty instances
in this book of
events that later
found their way into
song lyrics in one way or
another. Did you spot them? I'm
not going to tell you which songs
I mean. That would be illegal. Besides,
you might be able to find even more than
I have. What we've been doing up here hasn't
been 'waste management' or 'tidying' or evaluating
possessions to check whether they 'bring us joy'
or not – we've been handling the raw materials.
The Good Pop & the Bad Pop. & it all counts –
ALL of it. & it can be made into whatever you want
it to be. That's what I did.

Now it's your turn.

Thanks for your help.

That's enough for now.

Goodnight.

CREDITS

All photographs by Jarvis Cocker unless otherwise noted.

Family Ektachrome transparencies taken by Hugh Hoyland.

Page 18 – "Annie's Song", written by John Denver, published by Cherry Lane Music
Page 58/59 – unknown school photographer
Page 60 – unknown school photographer
Page 75 – Christine Cocker
Page 92 – Saskia Cocker
Page 97 – Saskia Cocker
Page 115 – unknown school photographer
Page 123 – "If I Never Get to Love You" sung by Marianne Faithfull, written by Burt Bacharach & Hal David.
Page 134 – "Banjo" written & performed by Leonard Cohen, published by Sony/ATV.
Page 136/137 – Alex Sturrock
Page 138 – Saskia Cocker
Page 156/157 – Homer Sykes
Page 159 – Kevin Cummins
Page 178 – unknown school photographer
Page 180 – Nick Taylor
Page 193 – David Gillott
Page 200 – M.A.W Allott
Page 204 – Martin Lacey
Page 210 – unknown street photographer
Page 212 – unknown street photographer
Page 215 – Martin Lacey
Page 221 – Chris Wicks
Page 224 – Dave Simmons
Page 236 – Sheffield Newspapers
Page 245 – David Bocking
Page 250 – "Tomorrow Never Knows", Words and Music

Page 275 – Saskia Cocker
Page 287 – David Bocking
Page 288 – David Bocking
Page 291 – David Bocking
Page 292/293 – David Bocking
Page 294 – David Bocking
Page 297 – David Bocking
Page 298 – David Bocking
Page 303 – David Bocking
Page 320 – unknown wedding photographer
Page 324 – David Bocking

If I have missed anyone out please accept my apologies &
get in touch.

A playlist featuring music referred to in the text is available
to listen to at:https://ffm.to/goodpopbadpop

THANKS

This book wouldn't exist if not for my literary agent Mónica Carmona. She believed I could write a book long before I believed it myself. Muchas gracias, Mónica.

Michal Shavit, my editor at Jonathan Cape, & her amazing team – including Bea Hemming & Ana Fletcher – guided me through the writing process, gave encouragement when it was needed & really helped shape the material.

Julian House was the perfect designer for this book. We share a love for the publishing experiments of a certain era. Julian was able to take those reference points & craft something that is both a pleasure to read & beautiful to look at.

Thanks also to all the people who read parts of this book at various stages of its development: Jeannette Lee, Raina Lampkins Fielder, Mary Franklin, Antony Genn, Harland Miller, Douglas Coupland, Steve Albini, Kim Sion, Chilly Gonzales.

There are also many people who helped track down photos, objects, gave legal advice, gave support exactly when it was required. Thanks to: (in no particular order)
Alison Davies
Jill Taylor
Jonny Trunk
Mr Gazoline
Sam Knee
Sheffield Tape Archive
Pulp Wiki
Shumon Basar

Christine Connolly
Saskia Renshaw
Randall Poster
Janet Hicks
Geoff Travis
Mog Yoshihara
Kelly Kiley
Ben Ayres
Lisa Goodall
Martin Lacey
David Bocking
Sheffield City Archives
Adam Dineen
Simon Esplen
Mick Jarvis
Dave Simmons
Tim Knebel
Jane Salt
Giles Bosworth
Joel Tomlin
Felicitas Aga
Richard Hawley
John Best
Polly Birkbeck
Meghan Currier
John Roddison
Lucy Suarez
Patsy Winkelman

& thanks finally to you, dear reader, for your invaluable
assistance in this ongoing project of self-excavation.